BONHOMIE & OTHER WRITINGS

BY HOWARD SLATER

Mute

© 2011 Mute Publishing

Acknowledgements:
Thanks and an appreciation of support are due to the following publications and initiatives in which some of these writings first appeared and were developed: Copenhagen Free University, Datacide, Difficult Fun Records, Dysphasia Press, Mute, Night Class, Ourganisation, School of Walls and Space, Variant. Thanks also due to Josephine Berry Slater, Pauline van Morik Broekmann, Raquel Perez de Eulate, Paul Graham, Caroline Heron, Anthony Iles, Mira Mattar, Simon Worthington.

Mute Books
46 Lexington Street
London W1F 0LP
UK

www.metamute.org
mute@metamute.org

Front cover image:
Joen Vedel, Photo-Booth Heart, 2010

ISBN: 978-1-906496-72-2

Mute gratefully acknowledges the support of Arts Council England

CONTENTS

From Exodus to Species-Being 4

The Secessionist Outernational - Hello The Err 17

Poetry and Self Exile 24

Convergent Suggestion 35

Infinite Dialectic 42

Modest Narcissus 46

Downcline 50

Burdened by the Absence of the Billions 53

Anomie/Bonhomie: Notes Towards The
'Affective Classes' 68

Real Phôné 135

Two Untitled Poems 147

FROM EXODUS TO SPECIES-BEING

> We had seen thousands of people that day. They were fleeing the world. We were advancing into it
> – Kenneth Patchen

> *Nous sommes tous des émigrés*
> – Henri Chopin

The theory of exodus as popularised by such writers as Paolo Virno comes from everywhere and every time. It is enmeshed with mass migration, forced and voluntary... from the field to the factory, from home to homestead, from the whipping lands to the promised lands. It is there as a practice in the Caribbean Maroon communities of escaped slaves, amidst the wagon trains, on St George's Hill, in the bongos of Cocpit country, on pirate islands, in the sign language of hobo camps and in the concrete coming-to-expression of social production that were the workers' councils. Each and every time it posits fight as flight, improvisation rather than virtuosity, socialising rather than politicising. 'Engaged withdrawal', as Paolo Virno calls it, is not an act of self-salvation, but an embracing of risk and alterity that is the minimum effort demanded of even the most informal of constituting initiatives. Exodus is an attempt to build community, to find the species-being in us all, to restore some sociality to social relations, whilst reminding those 'left behind' of the inherent laziness of their hard work; the expropriation of their own voice sold back to them as a shutdown culture of vicariousness and as a 'socially engaged' politics befitting the ongoing bourgeois civil war. Exodus is the moment of foundations, a space-time construct of the utopian imagination whereby poetasters abandon words and build buildings. It is to embrace the bruises and buckles of identity and fashion from them – from self-abandonment, from self-exile – the possibility of new premises from which to begin to be species-beings. Exodus, far from being an end-in-itself is only the minutest of beginnings or, as James Joyce has written, 'Be who, farther potential.'[1]

Seen from across the escarpments and blind alleys of history the subject of antagonism has shifted its shape. If capital can change its form then its combatants, to be effective, know they must change theirs. What better way to change shape than to be among the migrants, to be self-exiled from state, sovereignty and identity, to know that freedom is not in the ease of choice, not in the possessions that can be legally impounded by recidivist statutes, but that it is something that is made together. As the slave revolt leader José Dolores says in Pontecorvo's *Burn!*, 'If a man gives you freedom it is not freedom. Freedom is something you must take.' Exodus is the creation of freedom as a practice: a reappropriation of social wealth – surplus, abundance... these are the economic determinants of exodus. To be given freedom, to be given rights, human rights that sanction and give rise to inhuman acts, is to inhabit structures without knowing how they arose to arouse us. This is a puppeteer politics. Thus democracy, inspirer of the social pessimism of 'silent majorities', comes to be about accumulation, included and excluded numbers, optimum levels, balance of forces, defensiveness. To 'leave' such a set-up is not to escape it, it is to put it into such sharp relief that it pierces our skin from within. This demands qualitative relational changes, experiential experiments, an aesthetics of the common. As David Cooper has said: 'We have to trace what the person does with what is done to him, what he makes of what he is made of.'[2] The attempt to do this is in itself an exodus, a living culture that has always, without knowingness, been practiced as an ontological production. Exodus is about how to live on a rocking ship, under a train, in a burning oil field, in a paid-by-the-hour limbo.

---

1   James Joyce, *Finnegans Wake*, Harmondsworth: Penguin, 1992, p.115.
2   David Cooper, *The Language of Madness*, Harmondsworth: Pelican, 1980, p.38.

The days of massification are over. Only the historic party survives, the historic party of exodus: the dividual conjunction points of mass minorities. If the guarantees of wage labour have gone, so too have the guarantees that something approximating our demands will be met. In such days as these, where the confidence to demand is disappearing into the foiled expectation of receiving by right, we will be protected but at the cost of a mass individualisation, an identitarian lockdown of perpetual indebtedness that not just management lackeys know how to operate: the withdrawal of even the semblance of warmth from the fraternising command of buying and selling. This guilt factory, in which passion is seen as violence and through which imagination is mediated into standards, was a core trap of the Workers' Movement as invested in the institutions of its equilibrating counter-power; a trap that led to an 'abstract knowledge', that, smitten by defensive procedures and the reduction of expression to representation, couldn't enable us to get beyond a 'formal identity' of 'the worker' and his/her responsibilisation to the edicts of substitute bosses. The 'strategy of refusal', the anti-work struggles of the '70s that were carried out against the father-tribunes of the Workers' Movement who had their abstract knowledge to trade and preserve, led not only to the auto-dissipation of a classical working class no longer willing to identify with the job, but also, at an escaped and once imperceptible level, to a collective positing of a 'living labour' outside 'production proper' as an indicator of antagonism (cf. the living cultures of working class punk bands and reggae's mutations). Since this point, the Workers' Movement has been the main proponent of a nostalgic image of the working class; an image frozen in time whose positive punctum continues to be the revelation of wage labour as slavery, as a deportation from life. The Worker's Movement never overcame its distaste for a sub-proletariat that, realistically discouraged by a political practice that approximates a Punch & Judy show, lives in a kind of internal exile divorced from the means of expressive production and prone to implosive violence. But it never trusted 'living labour' either.

When Marx offered living labour as 'labour which is still objectifying itself, labour as subjectivity'[3], he perhaps spoke of life as a process of becoming, an ontological production of 'self-mediated birth'; our enaction of ourselves as one another. Peter Tosh: 'I'm a living man, I got work to do'.[4] Perhaps, then, the subject of antagonism, the forces of communisation, lie within the nexus of living labour as that which is labour 'without equivalent', a labour of difference that instaurates a communicative vitality that the subject of antagonism must now work with and work upon. If 'language itself has become wage labour' according to Virno, and, with Negri offering that 'production is already completely communication'[5], then are we not in a situation in which language, long omitted from most of the analyses of the creation of value, comes centre stage not simply as a means of command, the 'order word', but as a communal material, a general intellect, through which we are produced and can produce ourselves. Talk of affective and immaterial labour, then, perhaps boils down to new forms and new stakes of labour struggle that, making what we are paid to say and what we desire to say a conflictual dynamic, continue the struggles of old in the realm of an ontological production that Negri has called an 'activity of transformation which the subject operates on itself'.[6] Such struggles, markers both of a deeper subjectification and of an immanent exodus, occur in a much less molar yet more widespread terrain than

---

3   Karl Marx, *Grundrisse*, Harmondsworth: Pelican, 1973, p296.
4   Peter Tosh, 'Burial' on *Legalise It*, London: Virgin Records, 1979.
5   Paolo Virno , 'Labour and Language', http://www.generation-online.org/t/labourlanguage.htm ; Antonio Negri, 'Twenty Theses on Marx', in *Marxism Beyond Marxism*, Saree Makdisi, Cesare Casarino & Rebecca Karl (Eds.), London: Routledge, 1996, p.169.
6   Antonio Negri, ibid, p.173.

those involving formal identities and representational parties. They are neither the privileged domain of a particular class nor the knowledge-object of a self-identifying consciousness, but ultimately a struggle to wrest sensuousness from its commodification (cf. 'war of the membrane', see page XX). As it is with language, the fact that there is a lack of fit between words and experience, the experience of emotion – 'what a difference between our fluctuations and the brutality of words'[7] – so it is with exodus: there is always a struggle to open spaces of expression and from these reappropriate our 'living labour' and produce ourselves as fully fluctuating singularised beings antagonistic to an individualism marked out as a personalised appropriation of social wealth.

The act of exodus flees politics. In so doing it flees that brand of politics that thrives on its separation from the social and which makes all subjects suffer the internal exile meted out to the sub-proletariat: an alienation from their own social force, including and increasingly a force of language as raw material, which become an object of mediation and of management (an anti-social behaviour order for swearing in public is not too far removed from being forced to answer the phone with the 'corporate response'). This politics proceeds by an abstract knowledge – articulated in sales patter, political spin and procedural dogmas – that is never interrupted by sensual perception and which hence separates itself from passion and risk, from a communicative vitality adequate to species-being. The very vastness of this sensual perception – 'I have found levels in the realm of the nerves'[8] – its being a principal modality of the species-being, is what posits living labour – the

---

7 Isidore Isou, 'Manifesto of Lettrist Poetry' (1942), http://www.391.org/manifestos/1942isidoreisou_letterist.htm
8 Antonin Artaud, 'Manifesto in a Clear Language' (1925), http://www.391.org/manifestos/192512antoninartaud_clearlanguage.htm

labour of the senses, the work of sensibility and enunciation, the production of co-operation – as a form of ontological production. Exodus is the flight into the occupation of the diffuse factory of this ontological production; the restitution or re-constitution of communicative vitality. Marx: 'Social organs are therefore created in the form of society; e.g. activity in direct association with others has become an organ of my life expression and a mode of appropriation of human life.'[9] Those practicing exodus have no need to declare themselves part of a collective project because their whole basis is concerned with re-unifying the separations, the distinctions, that keep people apart, alienated from an experience of themselves as species-beings. The antagonistic subjects of exodus – those withholding their living labour – accept that their sensuous perception does not divorce them from thought but is thought's antagonist and adversary; it's what multiplies them, makes each of them a hoard, an infinity. We are already collectivised, interpollenated (!), and the enaction of exodus, the recreation of politics as expressivity rather than representativity, is what makes exodus and its concomitant self-institutional practice, a matter of what Negt and Kluge have situationistically called the 'production of experience [...] life contexts'.[10] This is concurrent with Marx's belief that communism is the production of forms of social intercourse: 'Individuals cannot gain mastery over their own social interconnections before they have created them'.[11] Exodus is such a creation. It can no longer rely on what purports to exist as the norm: the too clever desert of the real and its mirages.

Over the years, as inspired by biblical terms, exodus has

---

9 Karl Marx, *Early Writings*, Harmondsworth: Pelican, 1975, p.352.
10 Oscar Negt & Alexander Kluge, *Public Sphere And Experience: Toward An Analysis of the Bourgeois and Proletarian Public Sphere*, Minneapolis: University of Minnesota Press, 1993, p.8 n.15.
11 Marx, *Grundrisse*, op. cit., p.352.

been about establishing communities. This is still the goal but what needs to be avoided is the way that these communities have sometimes mirrored those of the fictitious nations by prescribing the essentialisms of a 'formal identity' within geographic boundaries. Such identities, with their enshrined transferences and rigid ego-ideals, come to be unable to live life except by reference to laws. Seeking after the human community they come to murder the species-being in a generalised genocide. 'Life producing life', the positivity of living labour, becomes, when submitted to legal frameworks, a matter of the suspension of experience and its risks in exchange for the guarantees of 'bastionated' knowledge (being told how to behave). Does this not create a situation in which communities become closed at the same time as they perceive themselves as the centre of the world? Such 'formal identities' create the 'self-identical'. Sensuous experience, our being responsive to sensual interruptions, to the 'realm of the nerve', can break this vicious circle, and replace its 'abstract knowledge' of legalese and lectern, with newly created 'social interconnections' that take account of the brutality of words, their unwieldiness, their being put to work as a raw material productive of alienation, their falling short of the expressive effort that informs them. This is a key factor for the practice of exodus and the new antagonistic subjects (cf. Walter Benjamin's 'affective classes', see page 68) for it is there, in that diffuse, placeless situation of striving that the presupposition of 'internal exile' ('unhappy consciousness', 'madness') has been left behind. Most crucial here is that the practice of exodus, to form itself into qualitative minorities, must take into account the 'transitions that always arise between feeling and speech'.[12] More than that, it must work with these transitional moments, however silent, however seemingly devoid of meaning – 'it would be necessary

---

12 Isidore Isou, op. cit.

to find importance in the least act of the least men'[13] – for these are the high points of sensuousness; the workings of thought breaking away from abstraction and self-referentiality. This is the sound of the species-being, the sound poetry of exodus that perhaps enables us to begin to make sense of what Negri means when, perhaps echoing Deleuze's 'the people are missing', he says, 'it is in the deconstruction of communication that the subject is constructed, and that the multitude finds its power.'[14] Its expressive power...

September 2002
(Slightly amended June 2006)

Afterwards

This text seems to fore-echo some later concerns. Here exodus struggles to express itself as an exodus from identitarian norms, a kind of psychic exodus that's later called 'self-exile' (cf. 'Self-Exile and Poetry' for the latter of which see p.24). This is as much about trying to remove our thinking of exodus from a topography: there is no place to escape from capital in this manner. This in turn necessitates the sense of exodus as a psychic struggle: the final frontier of capital is the psyche, and the production of subjectivity becomes an antagonistic ontological struggle. The psyche as the last space available to us? Yet the psyche is not an 'interior core' but that which is forming in relation to sensual perception. Hence my more recent concern with the 'war at the membrane' expressed above as the struggle 'to wrest sensuousness from its commodification.'

---

13 Kenneth Patchen, *Sleepers Awake*, New York: New Directions Books, 1969, p.55.
14 Negri, op. cit., p.160.

Commodified senses produce and reproduce increasingly alienated and operational forms of relation. Marx: 'the only force bringing them together and putting them into relation with each other is the selfishness, the gain and private interest of each [...] no one worries about the others.'[15] Whilst Marx had in mind here the relation between buyers and sellers of labour power, has it not always been a matter that this callousness, this 'asocial sociality' is the relational norm?

As if to offset the sense of 'self-exile' as something purely personal I am at pains (as I will be later) to have exodus be a collective practice. The very notion of species-being implies this sense of collectivity. Being singular plural: 'being cannot be anything but being-with-one-another' says Jean-Luc Nancy.[16] But, the title of this old text – 'from exodus to species-being' – seems to be suggesting that the two are separated. Maybe it's more that they were separated in the then prevailing discourse of exodus and the title is rather saying 'this is what exodus is for'; the process of exodus has as its goal the beginnings of a life shared between species-beings. The process of exodus then is as much about the 'with' and how we are 'with' others and how we could be 'with' others if it wasn't for social relations determined by capital's need for valorisation.

So, this old text also persists with the necessity for a change in social relations. This avant-garde paradigm has become for me something of an obsession to the degree that I intuit the labour theory of value as being fundamentally informed by the sense of 'abstract labour' being that which socially equalises all forms of labour, thus bringing them into asocial relation with one another. Relation, as a form of mediation, could be

---

15 Karl Marx, *Capital Volume 1*, http://www.marxists.org/archive/marx/works/1867-c1/ch06.htm
16 Jean-Luc Nancy, *Being Singular Plural*, Stanford: Stanford University Press, 2000, p.36-37.

at the basis of value. In this way, and bearing in mind 'asocial sociality', it is no surprise that I have turned towards an interest in the therapeutic relation. For Dave Mearns and Mick Cooper, two therapeutic practitioners, this relation has three core conditions: (i) empathy (ii) unconditional positive regard (iii) congruence.[17] For Daniel Stern the therapeutic relation is the 'co-creation of now'. This creativity of relation is different from its recuperation as 'relational aesthetics' not simply in terms of its non-spectacular intimacy – one that does not seek representational legitimacy – but in that therapy could be seen as the practice of 'dipping beneath the presentational level of the self' (cf. Stern's RIGs: 'representations of interactions that have been generalised').[18] The 'presentational level' would, in this old text, be something like 'formal identity'; the way we are supposed to be recognised and how we recognise ourselves conditioned by the need to survive in this world as pre-human.

There is also the sense in this text of an unnamed but, of course, as always 'new' antagonistic subject. This subject, formerly of the Workers' Movement, is for me more aptly, yet not in full confidence, best expressed by Walter Benjamin's phrase 'affective classes'. My experience working for a local authority has led to a complete pessimism in relation to an antagonistic working class subject: drowning in a sea of work, chartered by performance indicators, it's everyone for themselves followed by the daily exodus at 5pm. This experience casts doubt upon the continuing relevance of 'living labour' upon which capital forces an equivalence. The intensification of labour makes the variability of the 'living' into the inorganic, into a 'constant' capital shaped by the production of subjectivity. The Workers'

---

[17] Dave Mearns & Mick Cooper, *Working at Relational Depth In Counselling and Psychotherapy*, London: Sage, 2005.

[18] Daniel N. Stern, *The Present Moment in Psychotherapy and Everyday Life*, New York, Norton 2004.

Movement (what's left of it) partakes in the 'retreat of the political', a retreat that could be said to be configured by a lack of will in the labouring subject to push towards its 'autonomy', its redefining of wage-labour as human activity, as species-activity. Yet, as Jean-Luc Nancy suggests, this 'retreat of the political' is uncovering 'the ontological laying bare of being-with'[19]; the central role of re-forming social relations. A key to this 'laying bare' is language.

If language is a productive power harnessed by capitalism, then it is so at many levels: at the level of verbalised command; at the level of customer service; at the level of information and media; at the level of 'abstract operative rules' and expedient co-operative interaction etc. As physical labour power decreases in importance, then enunciative labour power comes to the fore (cf. call centres). Yet, language in the service of capitalism is a restriction upon what it is possible to say and, when we bear in mind the transformative, poetic, power of language, such a restriction has the recursive effect of auto-producing what it is possible to think and feel ('automatised perception'[20]). This, then, is the negative poetics of capitalism: a poetry of proceduralism, spin and defensiveness. The stakes for exodus (or for 'communisation') are to re-inject the communicative vitality adequate to relations between species-beings; adequate to the getting beyond or beneath or to the side of the 'presentational level of the self'. It is a matter of the sensual reappropriation of language, its deployment as a 'laying bare' necessary to explore the emotional fluctuations, opaque sensuousness and 'levels of the nerve', of species-being. We need to harness the transformative, poetic power of the 'fixed capital' of language to

---

19 Nancy, op. cit. p.37.
20 Viktor Shklovsky, 'Art as Technique', in *Art In Theory 1900–1990*, Charles Harrison & Paul Wood (Eds.) Oxford: Blackwell, 1993, p.274–278.

challenge the 'characteristic thought structures compounded from words'[21]. Such a reappropriation, as a 'deconstruction of communication' (Negri), is a laying bare, a sensualised reappropriation of language which requires that a seamless, informatic and protocol-ridden communication is undermined by a de-centring of its utterer who is no longer a 'subject of the statement' but a pre-individual deconstructing into blocks of affect in modulation. Stéphane Mallarmé: 'late in coming it seems to me, is the true condition or the possibility not just of expressing oneself but of modulating oneself as one chooses.[22]

June 2006

---

[21] Ibid.
[22] Stéphane Mallarmé, 'The Crisis of Poetry', http://studiocleo.com/librarie/mallarme/prose.html

SECESSIONIST OUTERNATIONAL
– HELLO THE ERR

Hello the err,

Threerrre's a problem in aimswerving your quests: coherence is burnished sick...

I/We/They are tempted back to mammyfestos filled with teste textual psychosis. The big boy balls of the prepublic intellefectuals are already too booted with cloacal-birthed words, but we thank you for attesting to 'us' something word-clad as 'experience' (= words are eezeh, but breadths remembered and insufflated among We/I/They is a challenge).

Let us try to ex-commonicate with some more ventriloquizzing:

'The drifting of sense and facticity relates to succession' in, around, that They/We/I feel a need to step away from the order-moats of discurse. Too much gobshite monadic corridoring can get you in a full nelson and some get quiet sat gulping and can't improvise no more and forget the power of vatic speech. So, for the SO there is encouraging music amongst us at all times: splicements, tempo characters, tonal disharmony, simple addition to bedded-in rhythm; such minor adjunctments to the lingvo that effect what I/We/They can conceive and x-presso. So, so-so secession is mad about seceding from the dorminant syntax-tact and knowpose: I/We/They want to Mean What We Say not Say What We Mean. Some poetic-affect be necessary for this, some *stravaiging* in n away weighless from the second-hand sense anchor of ideology to open something up, peel peer inside of its unsaid.

'IsN:t ComMMunitYOUTsideinTeLLigibiliTY?'

The repressed in language is the unsaid, but also what's forced upon us to say. There must not be a place for the repressed so it's relegated to non-representability (key to sucksexfull secession). We're tricked on fear of reveal into believing the repressed has no effect, but it's a prevailingly subterranean process that needs a ventiliated space ('sharing of the secret'). So, polysemy is the way we take heart, materialise the unconscious, the unrepresentable repressed: it be slips, parataxis, public jestering, stumbling, mumbling, misunderstanding, gang slang, fecund codifics, dyslexic stuttering, punnage, plummage, ectoplasmic citage, silage. All this in place of delegated silence... prying politeness... the seamless consensus-say of the formalised rackets... and in place of the objecthood dons of analysis. So, the slippage of signs reveals the malleability of an 'in stone' lingvo (alchemical secrets ignite their interlocutors). We/I/They uprise against the censorious schools and the 'government of meaning' that plies ipse discourse & we self-institute as cellular stanzas (a group without instruments) to undermine that self-aggrandising public voice that on and on drone surrounds 'a sunken acceptance with the vague reproach of the already spoken' (Charlie Burnstun). That's homogeneity kills it us. Shutdown of x-presso. Y'all stiff up in yr limbs.

> Awful bile also lassos our atlas
> Polysemy = multiple speech
> Collision of idea times for each accord to next

When we use normopath lingvo if't's not just fact-comhearse, ego-fellatio and predatory coherence, then it be a case of the most articulate being taken as leader, as 'personification of the anonymous'. The quanta mass con: one divvy indiv stands in for schollective and all the lots hide the ego-mirror stansions. But for the crystal orchid, lunar dew constellation of SO, one of many such woven rugs, it's the polysemy of singularities the effects a psyncopated polyphony. Tight like a snare. So, SO = empathic instability, NOIT.

The System UCS, that motor of secession, is a crucial component of ourganisation: it adds up to a collective drive or an achronological emoto-fold-thought that's machinic; it be like the 'third person' (or in 'our' case, the eighth: 7 plus 1 = SO). This plus 1, the surplus of System UCS, the materialised other of our togetherness (actually allotted a swivelling chair role by Charlie Furrer), is presenced as a post-spoken preamble, but also as a constant auto-suspicion, a negotiable undefended self-consciousness. All objects of our own singularity. Any ourganisation creates these entities (hence our interest in ESP), and, in so doing, reveals why ourganisations can be come occultish (hence the link to elitism?). This is where Goad comes from: it's the 'third person', the hidden third, the third mind, the surplus of energy wealth, the institutional drive, turned into a representation, an ego-mirror, and turned against those UCSs that made it up.

So with Nitty Fred we're always killing Goad to attain the new being: social powers returned via sensitised alienation to the collective that bore them (a Re-Eden?). The plus 1 as this new being in our midst ('our' species-acktivity). Living culture, then, is it not this social creativity (singular polysemy), this energy-wealth making thousands of plus 1's? Is it 'our' inarticulate prototypes articulating away anyway?

Charlie Burnstun sez: 'A sudden accord/ conceals an unseen presence...'

As for exclusion: this was oddly mourned, deemed dispositive, by the failed epigones of identity politics (those poor thems that try to reconvene the past, source it, put themselves at the Omphalos). These reduced selflets, powered by an essentialist narcissistic fuel, made halls of mirrors out of ourganisations, mass generalisations, made themselves representatives dependent-defensive upon event power rather than upon the split, self-exiling counter-forces of the eventless droning bass. Their lingvo suffocated us under the silent wait of table-topping arelational victimhood ('equality of oppression' was their relational glue but this made us dumberer to one another).

To be self-exiled, abandoned, is not simple passivity, is it not to be realistic?

WE ALL LIVE EVICTED (sez Mike Series)

To cut costs we'll be spat out labour every time (R. Owl. Gen sez 'the sentence of death pronounced by the economy')

To have ever fuller knowledge of ourselves is a misnomer (we are incomplete, insufficient, always missing, ORPHIC: 'I, is another' (sez Rhyme Bo)

So, SO's self-abandonment entails…

                        crisis of expression
  crisis of knowledge
                              crisis of belonging
      crisis of legitimation

At all times, then, with these multiple crises betwixt us there's no lasting power for the very instability of each cut through each necessitates the relational bond of an affinity group without which self-abandonment becomes self-shattering (pathological, misanthropic). But also. Time becomes the form of our unity; the passage of time towards history becomes an experience that binds us. Synchronicity. Breaths are untied by their told memories. Memories place us in a diffuse expellation.

AN OuRGANISATION FOR THOSE THAT HAVE NO ORiGANISATION

So, the SO is an attempt to orgonise on the basis of this shared exclusion from the confines of those gorycats that art the tools of separation, from those enternalised boundaries that reify 'our' perception possibilities. X-O-DUS is as much psychical as physical. In this sense it is invisible, but it subsists and insists at a sub-representative, microscopic level ('a feeling for what's not there'). Such indiscernibility, exiting the event (= spectacle), could be seen as non-action if it were not for 'our' praxis of the least event (=exchange situation). The vibrational activity of breathy contact, tonal touching, gestures encouraging the least confident, the most inscrutably senseintelligent, are such that relation attains a binding, a 'convivial solidarity', in much the same way as libido cathects an 'object'. Such 'work' benefits from the porous boundaries of the SO as an ourganisation ('the ones who participate in it are not certain they have a part in it'). It is not projected into public event status but, self-abandoned into small circles convening in gap spaces, spacious slithers, cosmic slips... It reappropriates relation as 'living labour' (Lloydie Slim sez: 'try to live good in the neighbourhood. Humerceh').

EVACUATE THE EVENT : X-IT FROM PROJECT
RECONVENE ELSEWHERE: SMALL CIRCLES

'Breath... is about a communication beyond verbal language.' Breath is music. The speaker heaves. The throat caverns out. We listened to Nicole Gossard not list recently: 'The body interests me in its circulation of energies and the way it provides, through our senses, for a network of associations out of which we create our mental environment, out of which we imagine far beyond what we see, hear, feel or taste. It is through this network of associations that we claim new sensation...' Having longtime listened to the body and felt the resonant undulations of its emotive force (energy as orgone as bios as libido), these 'new sensations' are a way that we can speak of 'building drives' and, therefore, of not exchanging for value 'our' energy-wealth.

'Breath' becomes more than a metaphor for the semiotic of the impulses that the Polish Count and Nitty Fred speak of: a semiotic, an 'energy-wealth', each has access to at all times; a honing and assembling of instincts into drives (breathing freely) – an affective non-knowledge, a self-consciousness that, overcoming the mind/matter split, takes us beyond human rights towards the species-being and the dutiless vow of frankness that can't be protocolised. Let's be serious now: procedures aim to produce and maintain the separation between thought and feeling, they are auto-censorious reducers of passion, they are psychotic inducements that produce internal CIDs and remove relational responsibilities (orgonisation as administered division).

No built drive, no new being. If there's no trust then there are procedures, tutelary guarantees, instead. And, of course, all procedures need their interpretors and that's where 'parity amongst members' is destroyed: priests, project-leaders, idealogues… all power-crazed hopalongs who, alienated already (without taking the return trip), let reified procedures do the work (blind obedience to procedures is blind obedience to Goad – ask a camp guard). With trust there's neither transparency nor opaqueness but abreaction. As Divvy Coop sez: 'What a responsibility it is to make sure no one takes away our responsibility.' But caution: trust can be proceduralised. Moral imperative of Mafia Familias. Ourganisation becoming ouragonisation.

To end: we are not a 'people', not human. The people are missing. But 'our' strength comes from our dispossession. Everything is reappropriatable now. Blink, pores, duct, twitch. We could be the circular breathing of energy-wealth. Our covert discovery could be: energy is catalysed by a change of state dependent upon place and context. Energy wealth is what plugs into the drive of the ourganisation, assemblage of 'new being'.

> Class wars.
> Oil wars.
> Civil wars.
> Circulation wars.
> Membrane wars.

(SO: no more?)
(we've time to go)

Secessionist Outernational
1st of May in December

POETRY & SELF-EXILE

> Still today I am only counting on what comes of my own openness, my eagerness to wander in search of everything, which I am confident, keeps me in mysterious communication with other open beings, as if we were suddenly called to assemble
> – André Breton

It has been the practice of groups to expel, to exercise the 'sovereign ban'. These groups take kudos from expulsions, they rehone their position, and grow closer together. The one expelled is normally a one that troubles the group; the unconscious anxiety of the group is personified in the expulsed one. Cohesion grows in such cases because the group, based to a large extent on shared belief and an interest-consensus, can, once the anxiety is expelled, too easily continue believing and idealising in the same way.

The claims to collectivity of such groups, in neglecting the unconscious dimension of its 'hidden third' and expelling it symbolically, fails to be fully cognisant of the creative surplus of the collectivity. This surplus, a modality of the affective charges of any 'putting-into-relation', is the very stuff of collective production. Ostensibly abstract, this impersonal force, when recognised, modifies the individuality of the group members, making them both object and subject. Without such an individual dispersion and internal contradiction – which is the equivalent of letting desire diffuse through the group and, overflowing its bounds, animating its practice of sociality – the group remains at the level of a collection of individuals.

Here we have the problem that afflicts groups of all sorts: the repression of the unconscious dimension and thus this disavowal of the affective charge, not only permanently thwarts the collective production of the group but, a priori, maintains the individual member as an 'identity' rather than as a 'field of energy' and fences-off the outside of the group; it demarcates a boundary. In this way the group becomes a pseudo-collectivity that adopts the stasis of an identity. Its visibility is conditioned by the irrepressible joy of belonging in the midst of an alienating society and is sustained by the absence of the expulsees who, furthermore, become hypostatised as 'individualists'.

These principles of non-contradiction and identity that afflict such groups, that give them a pseudo-cohesion and a super-ego function, are a main cause of alienation and repression in that the affective charge, seeking a form of expression, is often subject to de facto censorship in that it can be tangential to the content and aims of the group. When a group has come together to combat the alienation of capitalist society, this unconscious identitarian and cohesive effect leads to a surplus of alienation, a double alienation that is mirrored by the valorisation of the manifest sociality of the group. A value that obscures the latent labour of the affective.

These affective elements become unspeakable because the group, emotionally unaware of its unconscious dynamic and, through a functional, aim-centric, use of language, lacks the verbal equipment to deal with these matters. It lacks the necessary objectivity that comes from a dispersion of individuality; a secession from identity, that allows for a de-individualisation by means of the group's 'hidden third'. Personal conflicts are heightened in such groups because the individual is not retro-activised as a 'field of energy', a cluster of emotions responding to an 'impersonal force', but maintained in identity. Information, as identitarian expression, takes the place of the 'expressible'.[1]

In this way then, there is, it seems, no scope to be alienated from a group that purports to be unalienated, that enshrines the image of communicative collaboration at its 'heart'. To be alienated from such a group leads to a vicious feedback

---

[1] 'The expressible is something that can somehow take shape and exist apart from expression.' See V.N.Voloshinov, *Marxism and the Philosophy of Language*, London: Harvard University Press, 1986, p.84.

whereby continued belonging amounts to a passive acceptance and growing resentment; ennui transforms into a narcissism of minor differences that, fruitful in other circumstances, is exacerbated by the unconsciously competing individualities of the collective that colour the atmosphere with the odour of 'oppressively disguised thought'.[2]

But, in the midst of such groups and with a will to remain opposed-together, it seems there cannot be 'other circumstances'. An implosion occurs in the ones whose emotional vocabulary has extended through processes of felt contradiction and affective disaggregation. There is an in-break of repressed material that reveals the fellows as gaining a disavowed psychic sustenance from belonging 'in-itself'. This reified sense of belonging, contiguous with the maintenance of identitarian perspectives, maintains the group in an idealist equilibrium, a steady state that de-charges 'fields of energy'. The group is instituted but not instituting.

The host group 'wards off its outside' which was internally figured by the expulsed one. It 'repeats itself without differentiation' and encircles its own raison d'être (ideological core) because, unresponsive to the expressible of affect, its access to the unconscious dynamic and hence to the impersonal force of its social production, does not provide the necessary nuances through which to effect a dispersion of identity (becoming singular). Moreover, this repression leaves the 'hidden third' of the collective production as an abstract entity that faces it oppressively. This abstraction is unconsciously recognised as being 'outside' the group; a source-object of fear that provokes a controlling impulse.

In these circumstances, and increasingly in the more informal groupings of today, there is, then, a growing practice

---

[2] Witold Gombrowicz, *Pornographia*, London: Calder & Boyars, 1966, p.59.

of 'self-exile'; a strategy of secession, dropping away, from the epistemologically certain oppositionists in order to overcome the recursive abstraction of 'individuality' and the concomitant disavowal of unconscious dynamics that are enshrined in the group.[3] This 'self-exile' is chosen in place of what is increasingly transparent in the host-group as 'self-exclusion'. The host-group, motivated more and more by 'ideas', becomes a protective vesicle that grows socially inept, de-differentiated, the more it hones down an acceptably denigrating and unenigmatic language.

The 'self-exiled' are those who, in the clinic-prison of the group, have experienced the dialectical swaying of being and non-being. Not meaning 'death' as such, this non-being, conditioned by the affective vacuum in the group's idea of itself as a collectivity and its increasing alienation from an 'outside', is felt, by means of repression of the affective, as non-being in the sense of frozen feeling. Without this de-individualising dynamism of expressible affect and the concomitant immersion within the ostensibly abstract collective surplus (general intellect), continued belonging is felt as both a loss of the 'group being' of the 'self' and as a hardening of a 'being-self' in the group. André Breton: 'this being must become other for himself, reject himself, condemn himself [...] abolish [...] to the profit of others in order to be reconstituted in their unity with him.'[4]

To remain transitive and poised between being and non-being, to remain potentiated in a state of becoming, to remain

---

3   See Tiqqun #1, 'Conscious Organ of the Imaginary Party: Exercises in Critical Metaphysics', 1999: 'To start again means: to rally social secession/ opacity, to join/ demobilisation', http://interactivist.autonomedia.org/node/3556

4   André Breton, *Communicating Vessels*, Lincoln: University of Nebraska Press 1990, p.137. In relation to 'non-being' Antonio Negri speaks of the 'edge of being': a poise between the past-as-eternal and the yet-to-come. See *Time For Revolution*, London: Continuum, 2003, p.174.

open to objective chance and the fortuitousness of encounter ('surrealist' markers of the abstract collective surplus), the self-exiled, rejected by themselves and on pain of possible denigration, leave the group whose inability to perceive, let alone articulate, the affective charge of the 'hidden third', means that the possibilities for collective requital and sensuous appropriation of the alienated are gravely handicapped. The vacuum of relation, mediated by information and individualised through the double-reflection of personal identity and group identity, has the effect of nullifying the general intellect as symbolised by the 'hidden third', and, through self-exclusion, reinforces a personalised pessimism about wider social possibility: the onus is always on the 'self'.

The self-exiled, in leaving rather than being expelled, may have been expected to remain and articulate their critique of the group. Not only is this not possible as a result of the affective vacuum that negates the expressible but, strategically, the self-exiled no longer wish to either affirm the discourse of the group or, more troublesomely, to assume the discursive power to do so. In silently leaving, in becoming the abandoner of the group, the self-exiled 'signify themselves as not being the source and the master of signification'; they repudiate this power in favour of a permanently instituting 'proto-meaning' (the expressible).[5] Never substantiated enough to remain, too emotional at times to speak, empathic enough to feel the ripple of miniscule gestures, the 'self-exiled' embrace the abstraction of the general intellect, the surplus social product, as an enigmatic signification.

The 'self-exiled' find a muster-point in the Secessionist Outernational.

Communicating by means of a poetic collision that, objectively abreative and foreshortened, wards off the

---

5 Cornelius Castoriadis, *The Imaginary Institution of Society*, Oxford: Polity, 1987, p.310.

valorisation of their sociality, the Secessionist Outernational, not so much a 'group' but a 'zone of proximity', an aggregation of 'fields of energy', participate in the 'unconstituted praxis' best described by improvising musicians.[6] Here the affective charge is not individualistically overcoded as a libidinal attraction (the reduction of affectability to personalised genital pleasure) but is enabled, by means of social doing, to open up a field of desire and proto-meaning that is wider than each of the participants yet, as the 'hidden third', materially arising from the 'intellect-in-general' of their relation. In contrast to such a re-appropriation of the ostensibly abstract, the abandoned group's pursual of meaning and the means by which to become effectively active leads to 'constituted unpraxis' and an accumulation of ideological produce.

As affective dynamism, now additionally propelled by the dialectic of being and non-being, creates 'experimental positions' of proto-meaning that correspond to the 'expressible' of emotional states, it becomes clear to the 'self-exiled' that the problem of speech in the abandoned group was one of 'mastery' rather than a transitive, poetic means of expression. The indentitarianism of groups, their enshrining of individuality, makes such transitive, poetic, utterances become indications of fixed, personal positions: attempted mastery. The self-exiled of the Secessionist Outernational overcome this by using the form of poetry as an objectively abreactive means of speech: cognisance is given not only to the alteration of position as an indication of affective dynamism, but to the reappropriation of the abstract generality of language. Contradiction becomes an individualised marker of non-coherence and failed mastery, which is superseded by a form of the poetic that enables the unspeakable to be said; intimacy unfurls from the edges of inner speech.

---

6   See, for instance, Mattin, 'Going Fragile', http://www.mattin.org/essays/Going_Fragile.html

This 'poetic' aspect enables the Secessionist Outernational to maintain itself as continually constituting, for it is permanently open to the outside, predominantly porous. At the level of each of the 'self-exiled' there is the maintenance of the permanent otherness of the psyche (the endowment of socialisation from the monadic core by means of the psychical agencies of ego, super-ego, id etc.); there is an openness to the 'tracks left by feelings', to the affective dynamism of relation as it is creative of personae that can come to expression; there is, in embracing language as a praxis of proto-meaning, an openness to the permanent otherness of the general intellect in which portions of individuality (combinations of psychical agency) are subsumed to become 'anonymous capacities of affection.'[7]

But the 'poetry' here is not of a formalistic variety. It is not so much a writerly matter of a bringing-to-expression within the confines of metre and standardised forms of sonnet. It is not even a matter of free verse. For the Secessionist Outernational the poetic form is the form of feelings-in-action, is the form of thought-affects (passion) as pre-articulations, is the form of the articulation of the enigma of the self as other, the enigma of the perpetual acentric motion of transitiveness. In this way the 'poetic' can be a matter of objective abreaction: the disavowed can find voice by means of an oblique refraction in a manner akin to a novelist 'fleshing out' a character, but with the crucial difference of being actually living conceptual personae that are

---

[7] Luciana Parisi, *Abstract Sex*, London: Continuum, 2004. These 'anonymous' capacities are related to phrases we have been using to describe the collectively generated surplus as a de-individualising force i.e. 'hidden third', 'field of energies' and 'intellect-in-general'. There is a non-human element: neither being nor non-being but a dehiscence of the subject, an affective force-field that, to echo André Breton, makes humans no longer the focal point but 'sensitive points'. See André Breton, *Prolegomena to a Third Surrealist Manifesto or Not*, Ann Arbor: University of Michigan, 1969. In this connection see Gellu Naum's 'condition of requital' in his novel *Zenobia*.

not prone to 'development' in a milieu but to endless relational modification in mobilelieus.

This sense of poetry as an 'emotional-volitional tension of form' means that the poetic within the Secessionist Outernational becomes a matter of conjoining the materiality of language with the transitiveness of the psyche.[8] The 'poetic' is thus not abstracted from its utterer in some reified 'art work', but becomes a 'characterological' aspect of the multi-contexed person, a temporary unity, a reappropriation of the abstract surplus of the 'hidden third'. André Breton: 'I intended to justify and advocate more and more choice of a lyric behaviour.'[9] The self-exiled, nomads in the ostensibly abstract social product of language, become poet-persons involved in a raising of language from its informational utility (tendency to become 'signal') to its being inhabited as a polysemous breadth (tendency to become 'enigmatic signifier' beyond language). The poetic in the form of the person, as human life, passes from sign-value to the invaluable.

Such a 'poetry made by all' is not solely comprised of stanzas and an always manifest meaning, but by unsolicited honesty, disarming frankness and semi-formed utterances. This means that the poet-person is not fixedly in an authorial position but is, at the same time, an auditor. The 'poetic' is thus informed by a 'sympathetic co-experiencing' that, with a vari-directional and historically dynamic relation to the latencies of language, helps to solicit the expressible. Attempted and unfinished expressions mean that there can be a lack of clarity and informational directness, an opaqueness that makes the utterance enigmatic.

---

8   M.M. Bakhtin, *Art and Answerability*, Austin: Texas University Press, 1995, pp.81–87.

9   André Breton, *Mad Love,* Lincoln: University of Nebraska Press, 1987. See also René Char: 'Daring for an instant oneself the accomplished form of the poem'.

It is these very 'enigmatic signifiers' that need to be repeatedly pursued over time by an openness to proto-meaning that itself has transformational qualities: the poetic as 'affectability' has the extra-literary effect of opening up 'existential territories'.

At play here with the poetic is not a sense of an interpretation leading to an accumulation of facts (group as enterprising organisation), but a sense of proximity conduced by the unconscious of the text that is akin to a transference, a proceeding by affect rather than any logical causation. The 'poetic', as the inviolable invaluable, which cannot be informationalised, becomes more a matter of an ability to 'empathise-into other states', more a matter of the 'desire of the other' as it affects its auditors with the challenge of the enigma. This willing in the direction of the enigmatic and proto-meaning causes signifiers to take on a radical potential: with nothing defined they have a tendency, once they are cathected, to veers towards the 'transmental'. The poetic in this sense could be said to 'open for the subject an access to meaning as open meaning and to signification properly speaking, as the virtually interminable putting into relation mediated by the absolute other of the psyche.'[10]

It is this 'absolute other' that propels the 'self-exiled'. The absolute other in regards to the psyche; in regards to the desire of the other; in regards to the surplus social product, the 'hidden third'; in regards to the 'enigmatic signifier'. The 'absolute other', then, is what is ostensibly abstract and what the host-groups, jettisoned by the self-exiled, are gathered together to keep at a distance and ward off. In this light, such groupings are means of protecting individualities in their identity rather than having being exposed to the 'absolute other' that is creative of haecceity and identity dissolution. This, to some degree, explains the continued fascination that the surrealist project continues

---

10 Castoriadis, op. cit.

to exert. The 'sleeping fits' (the group analysis of dreams) was a brave attempt to bring the social surplus into play, to make its ostensible abstraction manifest. As with the surrealist project, the Secessionist Outernational also puts its faith in an expanded poetics that through processes of heteronymy, and active attention towards the enigmatic signifier, enables them to reappropriate what has been alienated from human powers by processes of individualisation set going by capitalist social relations. Of course, the confusing thing is that this all begins with the 'unsurpassed trope of our internal murmur'.[11]

Secessionist Outernational
July 2005

---

11   Gherasim Luca, 'The Inventor of Love', http://durationpress.com/kenning/luca.html

CONVERGENT SUGGESTION[1]

---

1 This text is indebted to *Surrealism Against The Current: Tracts and Declarations*, Michael Richardson and Krzyztof Filalkowski (Eds.), London: Pluto Press, 2001. Many of the citations that follow are drawn from this book.

The surrealist movement, a reputedly avant-garde moment, has long been a covert source of tangential commentary on the organisational practices of intimate affinities, on the temporary homology of heterogeneous desiring-energies. After the mid '30s, when a much sought after rapprochement with the French Communist Party dissolved into enlightening acrimony, the various outernational surrealist groups have had cause to bypass a more formal manifest approach to organisation and opted instead for loose affiliations, for an ourganisational ethos conducted by practice and the materials of that practice. For the surrealists there has been no 'organisational question'; instead, there have been practices-of-life that inform the quality of relations-between. From 'fortuitous encounter' and the 'sleeping-fit sessions' to 'occultation' and identity dissolution, the surrealists have indirectly, by means of poetic rather than discursive texts, pursued a non-alienated investigation into the 'structuring power of passion'.

***

> It's only the incongruous relation of multiple presences around you that will violate you as you wish
> – Annie Le Brun

At the outset there were no pre-sets. Collaboration in common was taken as an a priori, an indicator that the dichotomy of self and group was a bourgeois misnomer. Working together as editors, magazines had already become group authored works in non-literary forms (questionnaires, collages); and poetic texts, aided by objective chance, allowed the sum of social knowledges to be appropriated but not possessed by egos. There was always something bigger than the group and its works, something wider and more ventilated than the individual possession of knowledge. It is no surprise, then, that loose affiliations such as these should be bounded by such an intimacy, an intimacy allowed for by the suspension of ego and a shared quest for the marvelous. This enabled the Parisian group to embark on the 'sleeping fits'. Whilst not a form of organisation in the strict sense, these collective trance sessions bordering on the group analysis of dreams, are demonstrative of the outer limits of any ourganisational remit: the abreaction of unconscious material in an endeavour to discover the desires and anxieties of a social life filled out by our capitalised existences. When Louis Aragon spoke of 'talking with the lights out' and of 'faith in the trance' removing 'the impediment of self-censorship which so restrains the mind', he highlighted that the surrealists were committed to a kind of public self-abolition, to a quality of non-repressed communication that, in involving 'the intervention of a personal non-self', gave voice to unconscious dynamics that not only traversed the group but the society of which it was a part.[2]

> This being must become other for himself, reject himself, condemn himself, abolish [...] to the profit of others in order to be reconstituted in their unity with him
> – André Breton

This aspect of 'non a priori' relation that extends to the very utterer of the trance (he/she is a stranger to themselves) is played out in the surrealist notion of the 'fortuitous encounter'. This notion also extends the sense of intimacy that is the supportive prop of the 'sleeping fit'; an intimacy with a modality of reliance, independent dependence, that Breton felt marked the group itself: 'a minimal dependence freely accepted'.[3] The

---

2   Louis Aragon, 'Wave of Dreams', http://www.durationpress.com/authors/aragon/wave.html
3   André Breton, *Communicating Vessels*, Lincoln: University of Nebraska Press, 1990, p.85.

meeting by accident, the encounter with other people who are not of your 'type', the sudden outbreak of communicativeness between 'strangers' has always been self-policed and warded off. However, the surrealists embraced this sense of random social pleasure and encapsulated it with the phrase 'unknown guest'. This kind of open and pre-disposed invitation marked the group's boundaries as porous. Indeed, it is often difficult – with all the group and inter-group comings and goings and their 'stellar friendships' – to talk of a group that is demarcated as a 'group'. Michel Rémy wrote of the London Surrealist Group of the '30s: 'It's more of a collective desire, not formalised but constantly being formalised.'[4] A perpetual constituting dynamic, befitting the pursuit of desire, becomes a praxis of being-together.

> We struggle blinded by transparencies
> – Gellu Naum

The surrealists, then, provide many covert clues to the problem of how to organise becomings, how to maintain a self-institutional frame for 'open-beings'. Once the subject is seen as a rhizomatic terrain, a blurring container of multiple selves, then the old methods of political organisation can be deemed prolific in their failures. This may account for the orientational tensions between the surrealists and the Communist Parties (not just in France but also in Czechoslovakia and Romania) whereby a battle between the party of the proletariat that enshrined a working class identity and the surrealists with their inchoate sense of the multi-centred subject took place under the manifest rubric of art vs. politics. The latent ontological dynamic of surrealism, the dissolution of identity as practised

---

4   Michel Rémy cited by Gérard Durozoi in *History of the Surrealist Movement*, Chicago: University of Chicago Press, 2002, p.308.

in the poetic dispersal within the general intellect of language, may explain why, at times, the notion of a 'secret society' and 'occultation' has taken a not uninteresting hold on surrealism. You can't 'talk with the lights out' in the afternoon sun.

> It is very difficult for some people to join. Many, who ardently desire to, never succeed. On the other hand, others are in it without even knowing. One is by the way never quite sure of belonging
> – Jean Ferry

What marks goal-orientated organisations, like narrowly political groupings, is that 'belonging' can be conditional upon shared identity. For the surrealists, who, in their quest for new desires and new fabrics of feeling, preferred affective to causative relations, it was a matter of these 'identities' being seen as 'sensitive points' rather than 'focal points'. With 'requital', and hence active attentiveness to the other, as a principle organising force of group relations, one can always be sure of belonging. The post-war Neon grouping express this quite euphorically: 'Here is a meeting of being characterised by the same lines of balance. An exalting friendship at the heart of an elective group which situates itself beyond ideas, beyond the gregarious'.

However, just as the haecceity of being creates soundwaves from the 'self', so too the surrealist groups themselves should be able to mutate, become imperceptible. This was maybe what lay behind the notion of 'occultation'; a kind of exodus from the repressing representation of a surrealism à la Avida Dollars (Salvador Dalí), a kind of overly demonstratable closure that belies the dissolving of the group-self/self-group in the turbulence of a wider, non-ideologically guaranteed yet unpredictably modifiable society. The surrealists, occulted, would become the 'unknown guests'.

Convergent Suggestion

> The one isolated, driven from the pettiness of his person, vanishes obscurely into the human community
> – Georges Bataille

The debacle of the defections to the Communist Party (Louis Aragon, Vîtêzslav Nezval), the Second World War and its massacres and migrations almost completed the occultation of the surrealist movement. A feel for absent comrades reactivated the already present sense of a kind of *infra*-organisation, akin to Marx's 'historic party'[5] that brought the absent, the excluded and the executed close once more. The sense of poetic receptivity and 'active attention' that bonded and emboldened the surrealists, their enlivening interaction with objects and text, acted as a form of emotional transference rather than as a knowledge-bank of interpretation. In the late '60s the Czech group spoke of 'transmentalism', which, in words taken from Agamben's discussion of friendship, is, perhaps, an effect of that 'otherness immanent in self-ness' that triggers the surrealist interest in clairvoyancy. Friendships, the multi-mutual circulation of desiring-energies, are, after all, a prerequisite to the resuscitation of the 'structuring power of passion' as an organising 'principle'. Mad love, mad revolutionary love, love beyond nature and oedipus, beyond two, for 'active participation in the mutations of matter'. [6]

---

[5] For Jacques Camatte the historic party could be 'this reach beyond the possible' that 'constitutes the continuity among the human generations'. See Jacques Camatte, *The Wandering of Humanity*, Detroit: Black & Red, 1973, p.44.

[6] For such mutations see Luciana Parisi, *Abstract Sex*, London: Continuum, 2004.

> Still today I am counting on what comes of my own openness, my eagerness to wander in search of everything, which I am confident, keeps me in mysterious communication with other open beings, as if we were suddenly called to assemble
> – André Breton

Whilst the surrealist groups can be seen as self-selecting unelective affinities, or as, in the words of the Coupre group of the late '60s, a 'non-directive collection of attitudes', what saves them from a narcissistic hermeticism is that the desiring-energy that animates the groups, their practical pursual of non-goal orientated passions, is eloquently productive of the nuances, the haeccities, that establish minor differences, delicacies, as propulsions for collective becoming. Perhaps, what underpins the surrealist project is the futurity of Fourier and his phalansteries. Here, following your inclinations becomes a matter of self-organising according to the dynamics and modulations of the material-prop of the passions. The refraction of such desires, through the tempered agency of those of others who are co-organised, becomes a means of grounding the possible of these desires socially. Such tangibilities can aid the push to appropriate created relation. The surreal is the pursuit of more reality...

July 2005

INFINITE
DIALECTIC

one and all
no 'and'
holes in each
animal gist
modified instinct
drive alchemy
neo-human
'I', an abstraction
'I', unreal
sidereal pore
cathected moons
nerve horizon
opening species
quazar orgone
again the holes
blissful hiatus
syncopation
tendon rhythms
us is as tender
mosaic tendencies
archaic whole
de-specialised
working revolt
forking twines
fortuitous encounter

Infinite Dialectic

non-seconded time
fallopian minds
dissected Rex
the breach beneath
abreactive space
saying sustains
unleaden
unstuck
word block
speech defect
beyond language
stuttered thought
gesture lakes
interstellar mime
replacement hate
cathected soil
return to forethought
sift out the probable
mine the impossible
defy atomisation
the universal 'I'
strutting fly
mind of self
spitooning pride

deluded hogs
convenient renegades
crap actors
idealist exhortations
fideist id
plunge upside
deracinate
crystal skull
refracting desire
node prisms
no necessity
scarcity lie
hierarchic fires
state spires
MP monkey
save hearts
aorta tune
anti-human
supra moral
aeon becomings
common marsh

December 2004

MODEST NARCISSUS[1]

---
[1] Impressionistic review of Claude Cahun, *Disavowals*, London: Tate, 2007.

Claude Cahun,
beloved egghead on silver gelatin,
beloved incestuous semi-lesbian and
anti-Nazi by fusion of circumstance
and implied politics.

Claude Cahun, impaled owl.
Breton's hope becoming unbecoming,
auto availed in self-exile.

Claude Cahun, uningratiating.
Your eye swabbed, you God!
Your womb scraped, you limb-bud!

Claude Cahun, you belittle God with your 'bitch soul'.

Claude Cahun, passer-through to identity's
void where the seeping grit
of bit-part ego precipitates rise up in
a base force crowd of you.

Claude Cahun, the void is the individual as essence.

Claude Cahun, almost literary, but…

Claude Cahun, arriving multiplied
at several margins at 'anxious dawn'
to make mosaics from the spin of the hand-held mirror.

Modest Narcissus

Claude Cahun, already posthumous,
already, before the ink dries,
before the mascara tips the iris.
You're a problem for publicness
but not shy of vanity ('ugly' is your verdict).

Claude Cahun, unashamed of conceit and
artifice, beguiled by your own voice.
Your own image tricks,
you assert yourself to smithereens.

Claude Cahun, seventy-seven years of
'invisible adventure' all accepting-of
and lining-out the mantraps of becoming.

Claude Cahun, the accusations against
yourself mount as you pass through
the first stage of metamorphosis:
your 'appetitive self-consciousness'
is whetted and you're through to the
distance between differences.

Claude Cahun, the felt-sense of being
on the out ('a jobless virgin, a queen on
strike') makes of you a misanthrope.
But, wavering with bristling incertitude,
adapting to the moving floor of ambivalence,
you cannot be some fundament to follow.

Claude Cahun, you do not keep us others
within ourselves but, beyond your dismantled
being (embracing demise), there is an
erotic reversal and dispersal of self-exoticism.

Claude Cahun, the malicious love
for yourself wasn't strong enough to bind
you in any one image
in any all revealing intelligibility.
Instead, a praxis of spasms,
a praxis of organismic civil war.

Claude Cahun, that you abided by
your narcissism was neither of primary nor
of secondary importance, but, perhaps,
gave through to the grouped insight of a
tertiary form: 'the neo-narcissism of a practical humanity'.

Claude Cahun, becoming needs changes
of form to sustain it: poem-essays,
suicide notes, the other of the self,
the other self as mass, the group as ego, the
soloists in a lovingly conflictual unison.

Claude Cahun, this confessional form of
communism carries paradox along as synthesis,
as a sado-masochistic impulse.
Its surrealism resides in the habitual
extremes of your experience that are never
of common measure nor belittlingly unique.

May 2008

DOWNCLINE

Flat footed. Flat roof. Vertigo. Where to go now. Into atom mash at the foot of the clause. To disappear behind the veil of errant plastic sex. Into. Unto trapped pavements, cellophane sheets, cracked biers. Seconded to the ambulance of barren dollar tubes. Each one a fallen self circle, a ridden wheedling indwelling of despair. Can they catch up these I's of another dawn storm. Will you catch up with your falling, somehow split in the silent star's dropping. Wanting back up but the imposition is to fall now that gravity commands it. Outside of you, through you, the only law now that can touch you. The force of bodies through orange-tinged air.

Nor turn nor decline the offer.
Orange.
Oracle of cranial crate asunder.
Dropping a plumbline.
Swinging as if suspended, supported.
Depositions in christian courts cannot tomb you.
Lines of phoned deportment cannot prison you.
The tone is cherished, wished back.
A touch to provide the wind of white silk safety nets.

Oh, how they fell. The fallen at first and always too much grief to ever escape the hyperthought that leads to celestial implosions.

Oh, how they fly. The flyers that never stay still enough to plumb the little deaths of their lithe over-egged over-aggrandising selves.

DOWNCLINE

White silk shifts nestle amongst the boulders, the paladins, the tin can kerbs, the uprooted tarmac. Coming into it now the flick-film of pacifying lies and mistaken assumptions didn't come down to a core after all. It will settle in a palpitating ossuary shower of personality change. One implanted narrative after another. A whole civilization of discontents flying the plumbline as the city awakens from a subceived existential skirmish. A battle has been won. From now on the lids will remain shut to the dour echo of profitably packaged hyperthought. They will open to the newly organismic geometry of crystal polyps.

March 2008

BURDENED BY THE ABSENCE OF THE BILLIONS

> But this negation carries within it a yes which is greater than itself
> – Octavio Paz

Over the past few years several publications have surfaced from what can loosely be called the non-Bolshevik revolutionary milieus. Ordinarily publications from such milieus can hardly be noted for their personal openness, play with form and stalwart exasperation with the seeming shrinkage of their circles. Such books as *Call*, *Zones Of Proletarian Development* (ZPD) and *Species Being and Other Stories* are noteworthy in that they seek, non-prescriptively, to provide grounds for optimism and fresh angles of approach for those milieus that will not rush to embrace them. A provocative theme in their approaches is the way that each reflects upon the modes of organisation of those milieus. Each has experimented with 'phantom organisations' – imaginary groupings of one or several that offer some means of conceptual secession, some means of supported self-exile from those hermetic orthodoxies for whom counter-cultural activists are, as 'culturalists', not to be taken seriously. From *Call*'s elaboration of a party of secession through to Mastaneh Shah-Shuja's investigation of 'reflexive joint activity' in a ZPD, could it be that these books appeal to those distanced from the vestigially workerist revolutionary milieus? Or to those convinced that capital's efficacy is, to some degree, related to its instauration as a social relation? Are such approaches, with their accent upon relational congruence rather than ideological purity, more attractive and less threatening for those put off by the over-erudite, the emotionally inarticulate and the suicidal militancy that non-revolutionary 'others' complain of? Frére Dupont frankly asks the question: 'why is it that others feel no interest for us?'[1]

---

1   Frére Dupont, *Species Being and Other Stories,* Ardent Press, 2007, p.39.

Of these books, it is *Species Being and Other Stories* by Frére Dupont that could be described as the most emotionally exacting of the bunch. Being, in some ways, an account and autopsy of disillusionment, it has a self-interrogatory rigour that reminds me of Foucault's insistence that revolutionaries of all hues ask themselves why they identify as revolutionaries: too often the 'role' is taken for granted. For Frére Dupont it could be more a matter of talking of a 'pro-revolutionary milieu', of getting rid of the identitarian baggage, moral purity and dysfunctional personal relations that abound, and embracing, instead, a manner of being that befits what he calls the 'for-human' of species-being: 'only when the left despairs of itself is there room for a vaguely human becoming.'[2]

That brother Dupont does not intensively interrogate, in an explicatory way, what Marx means by species-being, but offers it up as a non-foreclosed 'for-human' (with all the pitfalls that could entail), means that as readers we must suspend our yearning for 'received truth' and participate in the suspension of certainties. Indeed, there is nothing certain in what Marx says: 'Conscious life activity directly distinguishes man from animal life activity. Only because of that is he a species-being.'[3] But such conscious life activity does not necessarily mean theoretical work, but maybe means an ongoing lived antagonism between drives and the adequacy, or not, of forms of collective being. The presence within us of these drives and affects that cut across and cut up our rationalising and forecasting is, for me at least, an element of species-being that persists as a common human trait that ideological production cannot appease. An articulation

---

2   Ibid., p.102.
3   Karl Marx, *Early Writing*, London: Pelican, 1984, p.328. A discussion on species-being by some members of the Internationalist Perspective group can be followed at http://internationalist-perspective.org/IP/ip-archive/ip-archive.html. The exchange was inaugurated by Rose in Issue 43, 2005. Thanks to N for this link.

of the messiness of all this is a possible take on Dupont's 'for-human', and it is a messiness that Dupont does not recoil from:

> I cannot bear to face what I have written – bad faith dogs me. I have scanned through the words of course [...] That was more than enough to fill me with revulsion.[4]

Revulsion, bad faith, the fear of attack and of finical criticism. Is this what it's come to for us? This 'revulsion' endears Frére Dupont to me, and I hope in passing to take up its umbilical thread after outlining a little the eclectic content of this sui generis book. A book that whilst riffing, in part, on such currently debated concepts/practices as 'communisation', manages to come across like a work of experimental prose. The title *Species Being and Other Stories* is as good a place to start as any. Brother Dupont's mobilisation of a sense of fiction, in what is ostensibly a work of theory, enables a refreshing candidness and gives free reign to speculative and non-foreclosing flights (speculation and playfulness, and their attendant 'messiness', being often misunderstood and a cause for barbed comment in the milieus?). It enables brother Dupont to 'begin again from a slightly different position' and, as already suggested, to add his own take on the meaning of 'species-being'.[5] That Marx's *1844 Manuscripts* are a touchstone for this book should not be overstated since Frére Dupont improvises with this hazardous and dimly extrapolated phrase. Indeed, for me, it could be said that species-being is not to be taken as a past state that we strive to reattain, some sort of human essence, but a work of collective (fictional) production; a malleability of seemingly innate ahistorical drives. For others, such as the group around *Internationalist Perspective*, an interesting

---

4   Dupont, op. cit., p.iii.
5   Ibid., p.16.

angle is taken in their setting species-being and social-being in opposition/conjunction. And then there are those for whom the 1844 *Manuscripts* and musings around them are a cause of shame and revulsion at the thought of a 'humanist' and pre-scientific Marx. But, as this brother seems to show, there is, in the 'terror of the dawn chorus', in the value-imposed balance sheet of a life, always the sense of a 'becoming human' to clutch to.

In some ways Frére Dupont's take on species-being as the 'for-human' and the 'pre-human' is his tabula rasa, his beginning again from a different position, his attempt to find some 'invariants' or common human traits in the ongoing struggle against capitalism. And, who knows, to find a conceptual space for the working class after it has abolished itself! As with Jacques Camatte, the turn to species-being here is tied up with a sense of the formation of a 'human community' as the overarching communist tendency. A tendency that is counter to the reproduction of the species-being as labour power that this brother asserts is, in the absence of capital investment and with a prole reluctance to work, being left to the liberal state: 'the working class constantly prepares itself for its return to species-being, seeking its own level through this implied rejection of itself as working class.'[6] This failure of reproduction as labour power as well as the schizoid position of a class subject that, so the theory goes, needs to desire its own dissolution, opens up notions of whether the working class is still the revolutionary subject. I get the sense that for this brother it is the milieus that are the blockage in the revolutionary process; that and the ideological mediation, (encapsulated in organisational forms), that form a barrier between them and the Others.

That this brother considers that the 'for-human' is a more common form of being than the role of the revolutionary implies, I think, that for him the revolutionaries are blind to

---

6   Ibid., p.16.

the innate revolt of the 'for-human'; a revolt expressed not as a 'political use-value', but as a means to 'do everything to keep and increase our dignity as living things'.[7] That species-being is here made the synonym of revolt, and that revolt is made the 'essence which every human may access' may give grounds for a much needed 'return to optimism'.[8] However, it clashes with a leading question of the book: 'why does the proletariat not revolt against its conditions?'[9] In response to his own musing Frére Dupont says that these Others aren't inspired, that we in the milieu are solipsistic, have an insular self-regard, feel the individualised pressure of auto-culpabilisation and are increasingly negative. It's tempting to also suggest that the milieus (in all those separate waiting rooms) are so off-putting to the Others because each room feels, somewhat pathologically, that it's in 'possession' of the correct consciousness, the correct analysis, the skeleton key. Indeed, as a refreshing counterpoise to such righteous foreclosure, the meandering, engaging and almost extemporising aura of this book sees Frére Dupont later stating with nonchalant assertiveness: 'It is never a matter of revolt becoming the vehicle of a solution'![10] Revolt is not enough; you can't sulk a social relation away.

Whilst it is against the spirit of this eclectic and engaging book to attempt to place its 'conjectured ground' within a discursive framework (critical appropriation), I do struggle a little with the demarcation of the 'pre-human' element of Frére Dupont's take on species-being. It seems to function

---

[7] Adapted from an interview by Tatiana Kondratovitch with Pierre Guyotat titled 'Art is What Remains of History'. See *Frozen Tears*, Vol. 2, 2004. See, likewise, Franco Beradi who says ' the inhuman appears as the dominant form of human relations' in his 'Obsession with Identity Fascism', www.generation-online.org/p/fp_bifo3.htm

[8] Dupont, op. cit., p.65.

[9] Ibid., p.viii.

[10] Ibid., p.75.

on too many levels at the same time: as an exploration of the neolithic (or 'primitive communism'?); as a reference point to a state of precarity that is aligned to a human condition and not something of recent invention; as a harbinger (or childhood memory) of a relational existence unencumbered by the abstractions of value; as the persistence of the irrational and of a surplus; of the founding of human societies around death and ritual. The 'pre-human', then, is more succinctly offered up as an explanation of the 'destructive character of small group psychologies' (p.33) in that Frére Dupont writes 'up to this moment groups have tended to allow the existence of an untheorised pre-human element hostile to their own expressed values.'[11] Whilst the many surrealist organisations and group psychotherapy practitioners who work with the 'untheorised' and with the 'hidden third' of relational dynamics may feel a bit miffed to be overlooked, I can only think that the 'pre-human', in this context, is the unspoken elements of unconscious life; the transferences, projections and sublimations associated with group life; the persistences of affects that circulate between us; the clash between these mute feelings in search of words; and those 'expressed values' too full of the trickery of ideological languages.

Frére Dupont puts forward the tentative suggestion that pro-revolutionary groupings (already the prefix 'pro' is freeing for us Others) should embrace the 'pre-human', or, as my baggage dictates, unconscious group dynamics, in order, I reckon, to more roundedly embrace the becoming inherent in the 'pro-human'. The two, for Frére Dupont, are in interrelation and this is given outline in the section entitled 'We Build Complex Assemblages' in which he extrapolates on a phantom organisation called 'earthen cup' that has as its platform 'the untheorised and non-included aspects of human existence'. In this section of the

---

11   Ibid., p.33 and p.23.

book Frére Dupont sketches out an 'organisation for those who have no organisation' (Bataille), an immanent organisation, an 'associative medium' (c.f. surrealist groups), that rings out with both a poetic yearning and a declaratory tone that is vaguely self-mocking. He rounds off this nine point anti-manifesto as follows:

> Our purpose is to develop a feral subject, that which even if it appears under present circumstances, is actually determined out of time, by both the most ancient past and the most distant future. The subject earthen cup seeks to invoke has its hands upon the levers of its own transformations, its mouth issues a code of metamorphoses.[12]

The feral subject invoked here has echoes of Antonin Artaud (cited earlier by Frére Dupont), as does the persisting notion that earthen cup comes to embody some form of expanded theatre and that pro-revolutionaries engage in role playing games.[13] The spirit of the Bataille of Acéphale and the Artaud of Theatre of Cruelty peek in here especially in their similar insistence and interest in summoning up the beyond rational (discourse) of 'primal' elements.[14] Such a 'beyond rational' also surfaces

---

12 Ibid., p.47.
13 These role-playing games are not a million miles away from Mastaneh Shah-Shuja's notion, developed through a reading of Lev Vygotsky, that a Zone of Proletarian Development can be an 'imaginary scenario where participants within a ZPD could actively reflect and expand on the debate without feeling pressure to enact preconceived roles and positions.' See Mastaneh Shah-Shuja, *Zones of Proletarian Development*, London: Openmute, 2008, p.100.
14 Paolo Virno has touched on this too in the opening essay of his most recently translated book. Here, in talking of exodus, he says that an element in the dignity of exodus is entrusted to a willing confrontation with 'the murmurings, the dangerous instability of our species'. See Paolo Virno, *Multitude: Between Innovation and Negation*, Los Angeles, Semiotext(e), 2008.

in Dupont's 'feral subject' being 'determined out of time'. But rather than this having to be seen as some wildly transcendent subject it could be read, rather, as the furthest extension of a ZPD: the persistent proximity within us of the archaic and the modern; a marker of species-being.

Artaud, then, provides something of a prism for me in the context of this book; a prism that also allows us to catch a glint of Marx. It's a simple phrase but, as cited by Frére Dupont, Artaud, in talking of his prospective theatre (a combination of the pre-human and for-human, the archaic and the modern?), says that its efficacy is in 'compelling men to see themselves as they are'.[15] This may seem like nothing to revolutionary identitarians distanced from the Others, but its implication is that we can only see ourselves as who we (temporarily) are by drawing upon the 'untheorised and non-included aspects' of ourselves; the affective elements that seem not just superfluous to the grand theoretical discourses that we immerse ourselves in, but seem like indications of our own revolutionary inappropriateness, our revulsion to thinking in knowing-all tones, our shame at being determined bourgeois subjects. Frére Dupont: 'everything existent under the capitalist conditions transports value for the economy.'[16] If we, to misapply Marx, are 'independent centres of circulation', if the makeshift formula 'I=value' holds, then there is a compelling case to see ourselves as 'who we are', as who we have been produced to be, in order to partake in the

---

15   Ibid., p.15.
16   Ibid., p.63.

process of becoming human, of becoming species-being.[17] This is itself part of the struggle against capitalism that remains 'non-included' as such. Rosi Bradiotti has stated it starkly thus: 'one has to contemplate the unedifying spectacle of one's own failings or shortcomings.'[18]

Such a 'going fragile' is no easy task and it is to be wondered whether by 'cruelty' Artaud meant that a kind of 'autotraumatisation' was called to be delivered up by his proposed receptor-participants.[19] This perhaps leads us to the Marx of the 1844 *Manuscripts* and another take on species-being that, again, could be called an 'invariant'; namely Marx's assertion that, 'man as an objective sensuous being is therefore a suffering being, and because he feels his suffering, he is a passionate being. Passion is man's essential power.'[20] Passion doesn't really go out of fashion (well, not yet), and suffering and trauma are human constants that no revolution can completely eradicate. In brother Dupont's terms, passion and suffering are both 'pre-human' and 'pro-human'. In a touching passage he urges that pro-revolutionaries 'invite others to reflect upon the truth of their own personal anguish, and thereby recognise

---

17 In issue 48 of *Internationalist Perspective*, Sander makes the interesting point that 'the cost of production of the workers as a subject of capital, as subjected to the law of value, not through coercion or even the constraints of the need to earn a living, but in his/her consciousness, values, beliefs, culture [...] is a complex of issues that Marxism has undertheorised.' I wonder whether a hermetic Marxism is up to this task; a Marxism of the milieus that doesn't seem to take seriously those ramifications of real domination such as 'biopower' and 'the production of subjectivity' that have been developed by Foucault, Guattari, Deleuze and latterly Negri?

18 Rosi Braidotti, *Transpositions,* Cambridge: Polity Press, 2006, p.201.

19 For 'Going Fragile'see Mattin/Radu Malfatti, http://www.formedrecords.com/formed03.html

20 Marx, op. cit., p.390.

their relation to the world'.[21] Such an attunement to their 'own feelings of revulsion for the organisation of the world' may sound close to counselling or psychotherapy, but not all hues of these latter are bogged down in the individualising 'therapeutic dyad'.[22] Instead brother Dupont, in 'Letter To T', returning to his organisational musings, offers crucially that 'we must visit our frailties into the context'[23]. Does he mean that our frailties, our emotional susceptibilities, our suffering, our blocks, our confusions, our fantasies, our feelings of alienation etc., should be allowed into the pro-revolutionary group context and be seen there as indications of our endocolonisation by capitalist valorisation imperatives and not as our unworthiness to the cause? Frére Dupont: 'we are dependent on mediated forms; our subjectivity echoes, even desires, the reproduction of these forms'[24]. If this sounds to some like a return to Encounter groups, Maoist self-flagellation sessions or mid '70s pro-situ auto-crucifixion, then, it could be countered that these were all ideological practices that actively repressed the 'primal' or 'pre-human' element of species-being in favour of the self-protecting sleights of discourse/power. Foucault:

---

21 Dupont, op. cit., p.69.
22 Movement away from the individualising dyad and towards a more social and interrelational therapy has always been a staple of group psychotherapy, but many practitioners in the one-to-one counselling sphere, regardless of discipline (i.e. Person Centred, Psychodynamic and Existential psychotherapies) are embracing what's been called the 'socially positioned individual'. See the work of Gillian Proctor, Pete Sanders, Mick Cooper, Peter Schmid, Lewis Aron, Ernesto Spinelli etc. Some of this work is available from PCCS Books, http://www.pccsbooks.co.uk/
23 Dupont, op. cit., p.118.
24 ibid, p.105.

> the manifest discourse [...] is really no more than the repressive presence of what it does not say; and this 'not said' is a hollow that undermines from within all that is said.[25]

To allow for and work with the 'not said', the affective residue, gives an insight into a compelling nuance of what we are fighting against: capitalist valorisation imperatives as productive of a 'paranoid-narcissistic ego'?

If this all sounds very individualistic then we must remember all those revolutionaries suicided by society as well as the personal costs of commitment and its deliberate precarity that Frére Dupont touches upon in the pages of his book. It is this level of psychical suffering that goes mostly unnoticed in those milieus that reduces their subject to the condition of the physically and mentally exhausted labourer. This says nothing about the levels of despair that follow upon protracted exhaustion nor does it give credence to the potential intensification of such suffering for those in the milieus: you're exploited, you know it, and worse you feel it, but you cannot manifest these feelings in the prevailing language of the milieus. If 'I=value', if value is breath, then, in the depths of a psychical suffering you can become intra-alienated; the relations between your own modalities breakdown in the generalised equivalent of a 'self' that cannot become, that cannot risk its own difference. This makes us ripe not only to conform to the social situation as it is, but to submit to the 'unmessy' orthodoxies of the revolutionary milieus for the want of anything more effectively and affectively engaging on a variety of 'pro-human' levels.

And yet, there is, I feel, something pulsing and inchoate that is being brought slowly to expression in both this book and the others cited at the beginning of this review-article. Before

---

25 Michel Foucault, *Archeology of Knowledge,* London: Routledge, 1995, p.25.

Anomie/Bonhomie & Other Writings

drawing upon these sources it is useful to consider again the Marx quote above. Here, albeit before he embarks on his critique of political economy, Marx does not reduce the species-being to 'labour', but to passion and suffering, i.e. an opening out of species-being and not a reduction to one of its many (potential) facets. So what happens if we couple this to the phrase 'affective classes' reportedly uttered by Walter Benjamin during a trip to Paris in 1935? Amidst all the taxonomies and re-writes of class as a precariat, cognitariat, multitude, entrepreneuriat etc, this phrase of Benjamin's remains for me the most provocative of the lot. What did he mean by this phrase that he didn't explore for himself but which was reported and glossed for us by Pierre Klossowski? Was he outlining a 'phantom class'?[26] With this in mind, and inspired by the speculative tenor of Frére Dupont, yet with my own feelings of revulsion at adding to the list, could it be offered that the working classes are being recomposed as affective classes? What would this entail? A Fourierist notion of eroticised and pleasurable work? An appeal to the cracked up to unite? A suggested point of convergence around a species-activity informed by desiring-production? A reappropriation of

---

26 'Pierre Klossowski, 'Entre Marx et Fourier', extracted by Denis Hollier (Ed.) in the appendices of *College of Sociology*, Minneapolis: University of Minnesota Press, 1988, p.389.The phrase 'affective classes' is reported as arising when Benjamin was pressed by members of the College of Sociology to describe his take on a 'phalansterian revival' (i.e. a reassessment of Charles Fourier's utopian ideas). Klossowski reports: 'Sometimes he talked about it to us as if it were something "esoteric", simultaneously "erotic and artisanal", underlying his explicit Marxist conceptions. Having the means of production in common would permit substituting for the abolished classes a redistribution of society into affective classes. A freed industrial production, instead of mastering affectivity, would expand its forms and organise its exchanges, in the sense that work would be in collusion with lust, and cease to be the other punitive side of the coin.' See 'Anomie/Bohomie' for an extended exploration of 'affective classes' (p.68).

affective labour? A more adequate response to a real subsumption marked by biopower? Does Benjamin's phrase, then, have any relation to *Call* when the anonymous authors have it that the Party 'could be nothing but this: the formation of sensibility as a force' or elsewhere speak of 'affective circulation'? Does it relate to Jacques Rancière's notion of a 'distribution of the sensible'? And what impact would Jonathan Beller's idea of a 'labour theory of attention' add to it?[27] A great deal of collective thinking/practice (or a good critical lashing) would need to be done in this area, but Frére Dupont speculates in much the same direction himself:

> for the left this recomposition of struggle into an intimate bodily reaction feels like a retreat but they are wrong [...] Revolt is an intimate related ness to the world and therefore most real at the level of immediate feeling.[28]

So, in the revolt against economically induced suffering, a revolt in which we feel, feel-for and attempt to feel-with (empathy), we must also remember that these feelings too revolt against their bearers, that feelings are in revolt, that commitment is not guaranteed as circumstances change and the struggle to survive presses 'inwards' and exacerbates individualism and its pathological variants. In these circumstances, forms

---

27 See *Call* (n.d.); Jacques Rancière's *Politics of Aesthetics*, New York: Continuum, 2004; Jonathan Beller's 'Vertov and the Film of Money', http://muse.jhu.edu/journals/boundary/v026/26.3beller.html. Interestingly and in correspondence to some of the themes of this review-article, the anonymous authors of *Call* have suggested the idea of a 'human strike'. This has also been mooted by the Claire Fontaine group. See their text 'Ready-Made Artist & the Human Strike: A Few Clarifications', http://www.clairefontaine.ws/text.html. Thanks to A for this latter link.

28 Dupont, op. cit., p.68.

of relation, of being-with, seem to become of paramount importance; relations which go towards co-creating a culture that is informed by the 'pre-human' (unconscious) and the 'pro-human' (increased dignity of living things), that encourages the mutual disclosure of a 'going fragile' whilst militating against the appropriation for value of our sensual bodies' capacity for suffering and passion (capital makes money out of our death and our exuberant 'vital force'). Affectivity is at stake, the capacity to feel and be impassioned into revolt, to have feeling destabilise our selves enough to risk the making of an 'unnatural' difference, to no longer have shared feelings of revulsion informed by the operations of mass culpabilisation, by the inherent authoritarianism of language, by the fear of an inhuman, value-laden judgementalism of our worth to enterprises, to the state and, sadly, to each other. So, maybe, for some 'pro-revolutionaries' it is necessary to toy with that 'phantom class' of the affective of which Benjamin is still foretelling. Open up front.

ANOMIE/ BONHOMIE: NOTES TOWARDS THE 'AFFECTIVE CLASSES'

Upon the exhaustion of our chronicles we shall seem more naked than the arrival of the conviction of similar tentacles and clean winches for we are all within the silence of collapsing pain inside the sparkling tricks of our future
– Andreas Embirikos

1. The Working Class Goes to Heaven

> I learned the fourth estate was depopulated and the proletariat went from base to superstructure and how the university trained elite now carries on its work
> – Bohumil Hrabel[1]

We have been worried rotten about the non-appearance of the working classes as a proletariat. We have been worried like sheep about its lack of self-conscious organisation of itself. Worried too, with beads, that this (some amongst us would say) 'mythic consciousness' never even shows itself in the collective of struggle; that the practical being-together in struggle doesn't sustain the idea of even a class-in-formation, a would-be proletariat. Sector, sectors; never even no more the first move to the base line of a transversality that would be the first means but not an end. We worried, what with the credit crunch, that there is no summoning of the spirit of the '20s. But why would there be? The '20s being the next decade after the genocide of the working class? But why should there be? Sectional interest, itself the outcome of a division of labour (or over-acute specialisation) has become 'fractal' enough to make psychical blinkers for us all. So, we're worried to see lists from bygone eras that, when compiled thus, seem like another golden era and not the beginning of the end again. We're worried quickly that the signs of class activity are also listed and that these lists get progressively distant from the location of their compilers; that these lists don't list (as in waver) from the sureness that the struggle in question is consciously proletarian. So, we're worried and we'll continue being worried in the next bit...

We're worried that the class doesn't want to be a class and that the only ones who want it thus are those not from that class.

---

1   Bohumil Hrabal, *Too Loud a Solitude*, London: Abacus, 1990, p.22.

Anomie/Bonhomie: Notes Towards the 'Affective Classes'

We're worried that some of these people who are our friends (so much better formally educated than ourselves) have all the right political-economic reasons for having the working class as the 'subject of revolutionary transformation', but we are not too convinced that the libidinal reasons have been accounted for (have you too been witness to or even subjected to critical sadism, manly realism, alleyway phantasies?). We're worried that there is a 'subjectless truth' involved in the labour theory of value. We're worried, as interested in its potentially heretical aspects as we are (i.e. abstract labour replaces concrete labour as the content of 'work' under real subsumption hence there arises a diminution of 'living labour' etc), that this is a minority sport; a kind of one-a-side football. But, most of all (well we're worried about this 'most of all'), we're worried about how the working class, in theory at least, comes to be overdetermined as working class, as labour power, as living labour, as the revolutionary subject. Some of us who claim to be working class, we think without some kind of authenticity-aggrandisement (itself libidinally inflected), got worried by the pressure this put us under. Others could have cultural interest but we couldn't. Others could cry in public but we had to be 'hard' bearers of the truth that was our condition, that cracked us up and made us thin, that gave us 'brain cancer'.

So we're concentratedly worried about knowledge I guess. Its uselessness when it doesn't carry its own critique. What do you gain by being deemed right except the frisson of a little compensatory power on hearing the ripples of approval? Can the working class hear this rightness? Maybe it could have in the massified factory setting when a proximity to one another, a shared condition leading to struggle, made what was known a felt-known, a suffered known, a known-in-process and not an imported known ('workers turn back, you are like sheep etc'). I guess we were once in the lead of things and not on a leash made of flyers that didn't beckon us to our senses, but to our role as a prosthesis for the seemingly more urgent and universal

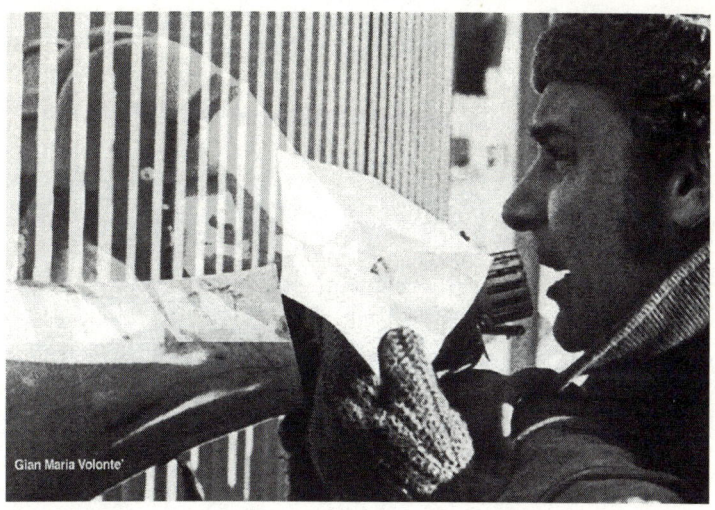

Still from Elio Petri's *Working Class Goes To Heaven*, 1971

desires of others. So, all we knew as working class is we didn't want to work for a living, we didn't want to be working class, we didn't want to lack the confidence, we didn't want to feel implosive violence, we didn't want to feel stupid, we didn't want the prison of our 'station'. So we were worried really and we really worried: we wanted to leave but we had to stay, we wanted to remain faithful to mass but we wanted to explore how the 'distribution of the sensible' had formed our subjectivities, how capital had moved into us to find something fertile for itself there. Affect. We were worried about the social in our psyche and the psyche in the social. We didn't feel emancipated by knowledge of our condition: workers enquiries and empirical litanies of oppression made us more worried; a worried that made us depressed. We wanted to do more with our nights than restore ourselves for tomorrow, tomorrow; the next day and the day after becomes pathological when the weekend is felt as being over on Friday at five.

We were worried that no-one except the dispensing GP took this kind of mourning at all seriously. The bind being a result of

Anomie/Bonhomie: Notes Towards the 'Affective Classes'

our being working class and only working class: affective pain, if it cannot be given a hearing by theoretically active communists, can hardly be communicated to stewards-in-unison. It's not militant to be 'sick'. Affect wasn't supposed to belong to us unless it was overdetermined as nihilist aggression or the 'labour of the reproduction of labour power' (a funny phrase for 'nurture'). So, we were militantly worried about the quietism of our colleagues and the supreme boredom, many moons ago, of our fellows in the jails of London. Eating pot noodle or sleeping by a stack of porn, it made no difference. Employee or prisoner: they didn't give a shit, they couldn't care less, they'd gone to heaven, but heaven either meant the return to de-dentured slavery of debt or the freedom to be kept alive without having to work. A strange heaven this where different forms of captivity could be exchanged, where different types of debt are being repaid; one supposedly making survival a pleasure the other making survival something to be aimed for, desired like nothing else. Both were forms of withdrawal from the stress and boredom of (a) an interminable working week (b) a continuously empty calendar. Both offered endless abstract time in the moments of calculating how long there was to go. But, if pain was never uttered in jail despite the obvious yet none too public by-product of being separated from 'life' = extreme inculcation of paranoia for those with loved ones on 'the out', the militant quietism at work was, when we looked hard enough and took it seriously, replaced by an affective militantism: hysteria of overwork, palpable multiple depressions on Monday morning, despair during the non-day of Tuesday, manic euphoria of late Friday afternoon etc. The supposed individualism of affect, while not named, was eminently communicable, affecting. We were worried that everyone was worried. We were worried that our desire to be mass, to melt-in with the class, to be nothing-but, to be a pleb amidst the patricians, to be in the social field without the prop of political ideology, to be alone, was taking its toll. We were worried by our wilful powerlessness, our masochism.

We were futuristically worried that our degradation as rivetheads and social servants was being recompensed into a structure of self-containment. We were bankingly worried that the less money we took the more tied we were to the job as if one more step down would be the end of all security, all future employability (sale of time as proto-entrepreneurial activity?). We were worried that this precarity also translated into a dread, an emotional precarity that very few amongst our educated friends could reconcile other than as some 'personal solution' of therapy. The few that were able to do this formed a moveable *sui generis* nucleus for us, a permanent community in absentia. Love came back that way and with it abreaction: this communicative dread became, just as in the office-warrens, an affective material that circulated amidst us and made us reclaim into expression our feelings (the sensual appropriation of alienation), made us affective beings no longer overdetermined as labour power and thus solely definable by books written for the dream of us in the '20s. And Adler, as socialist as he was, hit on something heretical:

> an affective state underlies class consciousness [...] this affective state always seeks to fend off degradation, it is impossible for class conscious proletariat to adopt an attitude of fatalistic resignation.[2]

Maybe not so much then impossible as now very probable. Maybe not so much impossible as a well-meaning defence mechanism permeating class mood. And so, we worried well that this 'fending off' of degradation may well be the last gasp of something and the beginning of something else. But what? The sharing of affective states? Fatalistic resignation? A breaking-point? We worried surprisingly about some statistics. We worried about suicide.

---

2   Albert Adler quoted by Russell Jacoby in *Social Amnesia*, Hassocks: Harvester Press, 1975, p.21.

2. Suffering Species

> Too much sufferation it's worser than hell
> – Johnny Clarke

The sick certificate supersedes the labour voucher. There's something hellish when our being contracted to be there interferes with a mourning process or a relationship breakdown. They give us a week or two if we're lucky. This falls on top of the run-of-the-mill permanent anxieties of being there to survive, to keep afloat. Added tasks fall to us due to the speed of information-demand, the intensity of order-demand, the incursion of managerial tasks, the porous boundary of the job description, the non-replacement of colleagues. Constant re-organisations mean that affective bonds that could reap solidarities are replaced by the permanent insecurities of staff turnover that are creative of isolation in that there's no time to get to know each other. So, there's enough cause for absenteeism and depression to be rife in the workforce (in 2006 it was reported that there were more 'mentally ill' people receiving incapacity benefits than unemployed people receiving unemployment benefit). It's when 'life issues' start coming in, those destabilising occurrences of human emotional life, that our resolve to 'go on' is seriously weakened. It's these moments of emotional meltdown that could pose a grave threat to the reproduction of the system. At such times it can be said, using David Cooper's dichotomous terms, that 'social alienation' and 'psychic alienation' become synthesised in a general but unnameable suffering that is as much a disavowed common concern as an individual pathology.

We wonder, then, if we're going to be talking of 'affective classes', whether there has always been a component of affect not just subdued and unattributed to the working classes, but as a component of labour power itself. When Marx talks of this latter he has used such open-ended terms as 'vital force' and we wonder if, when such terms are unpacked, they may very well reveal affective elements such as passion. For, at the outset of his project, at a time before the species-being came to be defined through its capacity for work, he offered, with more than half a mind on the precarity of existence and its emotional instability, the species-being as a 'suffering being':

> Man as an objective sensuous being is therefore a suffering being, and because he feels his suffering, he is a passionate being. Passion is man's essential power vigorously striving to obtain its object. [3]

Of course, the species-being could be defined from a number of different standpoints, all of which would be equally 'essential'. This is illustrative of the mass of 'powers' the species has at its disposal; powers that are, we would argue, ultimately aimed at the 'object' of becoming-human, however thwarted and perverted this 'aim' is under the value-production imperatives of capitalism. So, could it be said that from the outset, if there is this passion as a motivating force, an energy, it is a passion that leads the subject, the worker, to strive to be beyond himself, beyond the additional 'suffering' of wage labour that, it is said, can alleviate the 'suffering' by overcoming the vicissitudes of nature through the production of necessities etc. One could suggest that the worker's very passion is sought to be harnessed as labour power even at this time (it certainly is later); a passion that gives the worker a 'vital force', but which is also 'turned on' by its suffering component. At the outset of industrialisation, just as with the recruiting of raw village boys for World War I could there have been an active, passionate component within the 'forcedness'? In order to sustain passion (its energies and its auto-creative dynamic of becoming) is it that a certain level of affective or desiring investment has to be made in our suffering

---

[3] Karl Marx, *Early Writings*, Harmondsworth: Penguin, 1981, p.390.

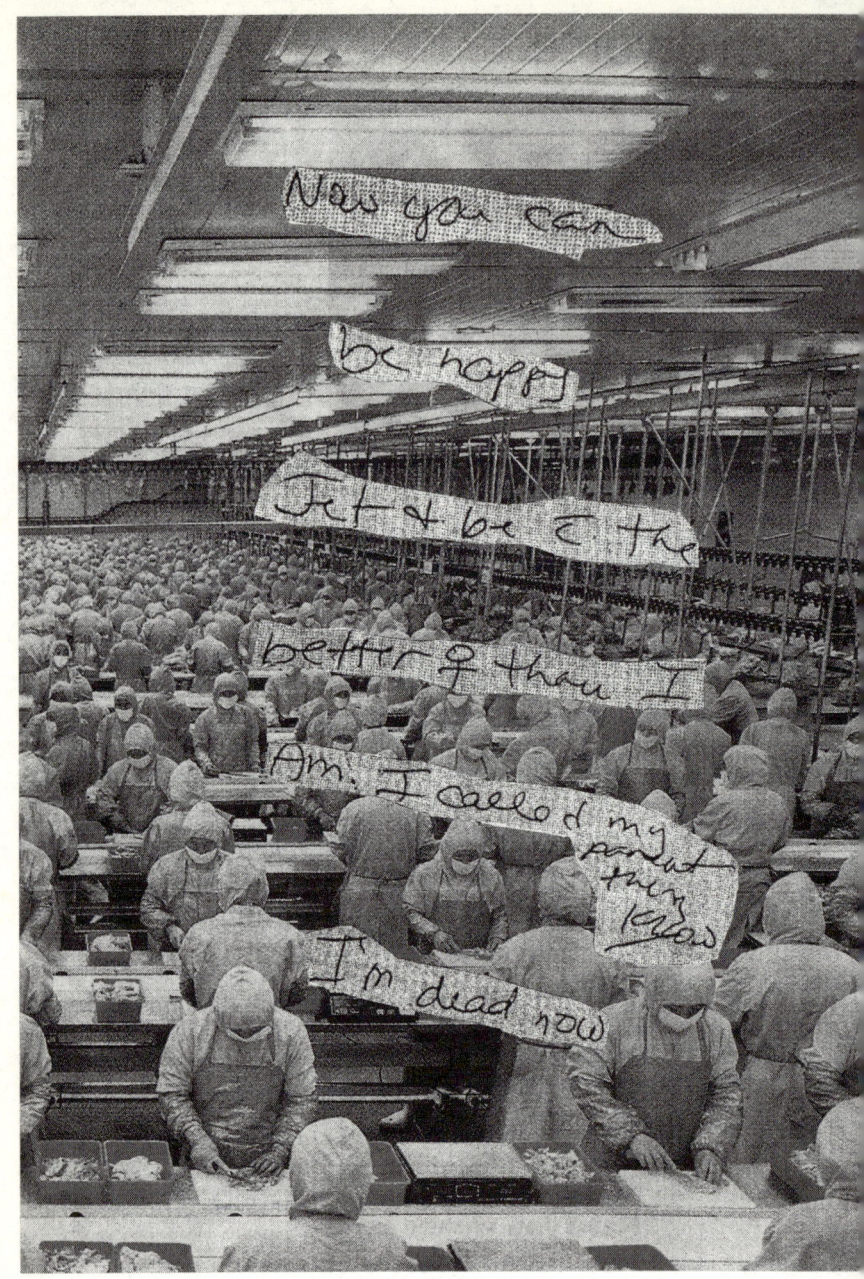

Collage by Howard Slater, 2010

and the suffering of others? This suffering component gives rise to the worker as being 'beyond himself' as a member of a class that suffers equally, that can recognise the pain amidst its members, but which can re-direct this passion towards overcoming the suffering ('living labour').

The Workers' Movement may well have been the vessel of this overcoming, this transformation of masochism, but its complicated demise gives rise to a hiatus: can passion sustain a cathexis of suffering, or as Adler puts it, of degradation, without some sense of utopian immanence, of futuritial movement? Did the Workers' Movement collude with capital in making self-preservation (the suffering of survival) into a passion? So, a class identity may be disinvested for such reasons: 'the striving to obtain its object' is not only given countless commodity objects to aim for (some taking the form of people), it was, more lately, with the extension of credit, given the option to work less and hence suffer less, to evade self-preservation as enforced passion, to somehow be working class no longer. Is there not also a further affective reason? Is this striving, as Siegfried Kracauer maintains, an urge of the 'group individual' to be more than a delimited 'partial self, to be more than the 'bearer of an idea', to be a 'full being [...] with multiple layers of experience'?[4] But classlessness or not, the existential suffering of the full being of the species – the births, deaths, losses, dependencies and relationship breakdowns – doesn't go away. They become harder to deal with the more our affective comportments are required for wage labour by means of a 'self-fulfilment' that sets to work the bios of the 'whole person'.

If the Utopian elements of the Workers' Movement aimed for an almost total alleviation of suffering they did so in the manner of organising proto-societies around not class belonging, but

---

4   Siegfried Kracauer, 'The Group as Bearer of Ideas' in *The Mass Ornament*, Cambridge: Harvard University Press, 1995, p.151.

around people's 'inclinations', around the affective dynamics of passions as potentially reclaimable from the capitalist goal of auto-purposed self-preservation. This may be seen, on the one hand, to be a denial of Marx's existential realism of struggle as passion, but on the other, it opens a space for a working class that was denied culture to acknowledge passion and affects as forms of energy and immanence. Using Rancière's terminology it effects a 're-distribution of the sensible' that opens up a way beyond the masochistic cathecting of survival and the concomitant basking in the negative that the Workers' Movement takes for its realism.

Charles Fourier is perhaps the case in point and it was, when pressed on this areas of his interest that Walter Benjamin, in a reply reported by Pierre Klossowski, coined the phrase affective classes:

> Sometimes he talked about it to us as if it were something 'esoteric', simultaneously 'erotic and artisanal', underlying his explicit Marxist conceptions. Having the means of production in common would permit substituting for the abolished classes a redistribution of society into affective classes. A freed industrial production, instead of mastering affectivity, would expand its forms and organise its exchanges, in the sense that work would be in collusion with lust, and cease to be the other punitive side of the coin.[5]

It seems as if this piece of Benjamin's reported speech may well be a shard of 'messianic time' for here what he seems to be bringing to expression by an act of naming is an immanent class, a future category to replace the 'abolished classes'. Despite the paradox that if classes were abolished there would

---

5 Walter Benjamin as reported by Pierre Klossowski in, *College of Sociology*, Denis Hollier (Ed.), Minneapolis: University of Minnesota Press 1988, p.359.

be no need for an affective class as such, is it that Benjamin is offering the affective classes as a transitional class in the movement towards a becoming-human that any communist revolution would entail? What's more, following Fourier, is there a sense that, in such a society the nature of work would change from wage labour towards a sensual appropriation of the affective dimension of a work for pleasure rather than for self-preservation.[6] More than this perhaps in that, as Benjamin envisioned back in 1932, 'work would be in collusion with lust'. But was this an 'envisioning'? Our experience of wage labour has shown that lust abounds in the workplace as a passion that finds the forms that are offered to it there: managerial bossiness as a sadistic drive, the pleasures of being acknowledged and appreciated reactivate the frisson of parental 'living attention', the tingling stomach and heightened sensual awareness of doing the illicit. In Elio Petri's *The Working Class Goes to Heaven*, this lust at work is ribaldrously given metaphor by the spunking fluids of handled machinery.

Such references point to a whole unconscious affective dimension at work. Some would say that such disavowed layers in which suffering is both cathected as pain and 'turned-into-its-opposite' as pleasure, is irrational and irrelevant. And, from the perspective of the Worker's Movement, it was just that: an irrelevancy. But, from the potential perspective of the affective classes and in the manner that Benjamin frames works 'collusion with lust', is it not a matter that work can be part of a 'passionate series' that doesn't have to take a masochistic form? 'Societary work', as Fourier calls it, has to be made passionate

---

[6] Fourier often highlighted the 'worry' attached to work: 'Far from being careless for the morrow, nine-tenths of civilized men are worried about the present day because they are obliged to devote themselves to loathsome work that is forced upon them.' See *The Utopian Vision of Charles Fourier*, J. Beecher and R.Bienvenu (Eds.), Boston: Beacon Press, 1971, p.147.

by being varied 'about eight times a day', by being given 'the right to take part at any time in any kind of work.'[7] A prospective timetable shows movement throughout the phalanstery in a way that not only gives its participant an overall experiential view of the work of the community, but as René Schérer suggests, opens the way to 'intensify the passions by giving them a social role.'[8] Work, then, as a sensuous-practical activity, disengaged from objective compulsion (wage labour), can be pleasurable. So Benjamin, via Fourier, hints at a 'desiring production' for the affective classes that perhaps Marx articulated when, supposing a mutual production as species-beings and not wage slaves, he imaginatively surmised that

> I would have acted for you as the mediator between you and the species, thus I would be acknowledged by you as the complement of your own being, as an essential part of yourself. I would thus know myself to be confirmed both in your thoughts and your love.[9]

Yet there is a crucial turn of phrase that Benjamin offers us. Could the affective classes be more than a piece of Fourierist exegesis? We think it may well have mileage for Benjamin does not have it that the potential form of production-in-common would 'master affectivity'. In other words this could mean that the utopian element of Fourier's scheme would be tempered by the acknowledgement of existential (social-psychic) suffering as ineradicable; it is part and parcel of species-life, part and parcel, as Marx suggests, of the dynamics of passion. Here we can perhaps see through into the future as it is now constituted

---

7   For a full outline of Fourier's musings on 'attractive labour', http://www.marxists.org/reference/archive/fourier/works/ch26.htm
8   René Schérer, 'Fourier's Rally of Love', http://www.iisg.nl/womhist/radsexpol.html
9   Marx, op. cit., p.277.

by capital's real subsumption of labour, its endocolonial move, its biopolitical turn, for it is not just material forms of energy that capital seeks but the 'non material' energies of labour power and 'vital force'. It seeks our affects and our passions and it seeks to benefit from our sensual capacities; to harness these for its becomings. The potential immanence of the utopian moment that effects a 'redistribution of the sensible' and opens up a horizon beyond self-preservation is, as our senses become forms of labour power, the site of a conflict or a collusion: the struggle of the affective classes.

3. Reproduction Something

> House – the place or space where a companion lover feels at home
> – Monique Wittig and Sande Zeig[10]

Developments in capitalism, be they the endocolonial effects of real subsumption or the rise of the 'attention economy', have made the Marxist conception of labour power more readily apparent, deducible as a sensual labour. The rash of theories that surround 'affective labour', 'precarious labour' as well as the notions of 'human capital' and 'semio-capital' all add up to a filling-out of what Marx could have meant by 'vital force'. It is the body taken as a whole: its affective and energetic capacities, its modes of consciousness and language abilities, its communicativeness and co-operative propensities, its erotic needs and its physical strengths. Labour power becomes bios. Labour power becomes demanded at all times of day. In other words labour power becomes one and the same with the 'objective sensuous being' and the passionate and suffering

---

[10] Monique Wittig and Sande Zeig, *Lesbian Peoples – Materials for a Dictionary*, London: Virago 1980, p.80.

Anomie/Bonhomie: Notes Towards the 'Affective Classes'

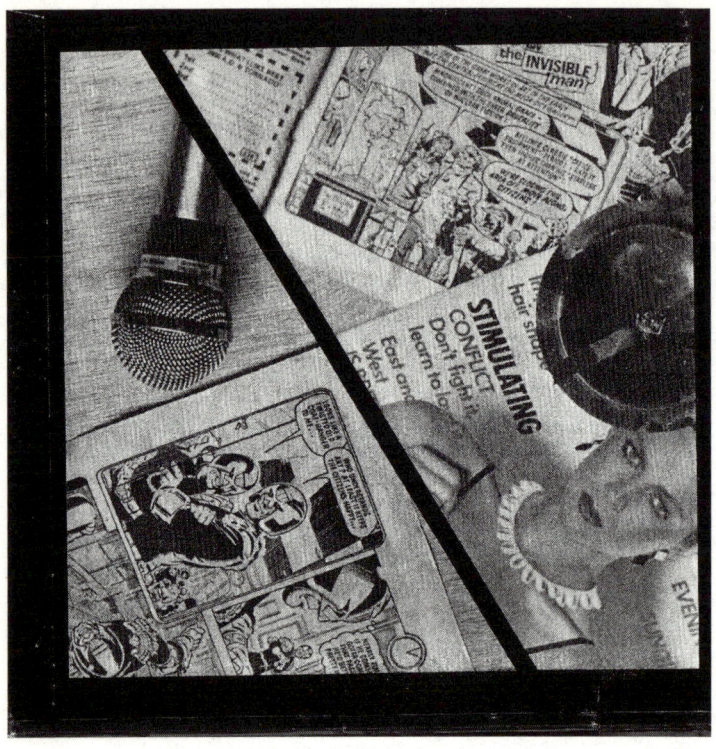

Taken from *Earcom 3,* Fast Product, 1979

energies that emanate from this. In some ways the precedent to this state of affairs and a key clue to the possibility of an affective class lies in the whole notion of 'reproductive labour' that the Women's Liberation Movement raised more concertedly from the late '60s onwards. This reproductive labour, in the form of 'housework', encompasses every dynamical energy that the human species possesses. But 'housework' as a phrase seems to be insufficient and almost insensitive when describing a reproductive labour that entails the raising of children as a biopolitical 'task'. So, this latter can come into conjunction with Fourier's utopian notion of a 'non salaried but passionate work' wherein a different kind of barricade is erected than the ones

Fourier envisioned. This is the barricade that has traditionally, in the Workers' Movement, been one that divorces what's seen as the social liberatory potential of 'production proper' from what's seen as the almost naturo-reactionary, de-potential of 'reproductive labour', of raising children.

The Women's Liberation Movement of the early '70s did much to redress this imbalance and, in doing so, it raised, perhaps earlier than capital revealed through its own becoming, the place of affect in the labour process. At times, however, the theoretical need to combat Marxist orthodoxy leads a writer such as Leopoldina Fortunati to situate reproduction as production-proper, to insert housework into the labour theory of value (housework as the production of a product called labour power and hence its being a process of valorisation), whilst occluding some of the other surrounding factors in this production of labour power.[11] Such factors she designates as 'non-material' use values (which could include the affective qualities of nurture, unconditional love, living attention etc) and which, she says, can figure as factors which are among the least controllable by capital. This could chime with a prospective aspect of the affective classes in that it is those species-qualities that elude control (or measure) that provide the means, the unassignable leakage, to resist the transformation of 'non material use values' (such as living attention, empathy etc) into 'exchange values' or means of valorisation.

In some ways, then, we could say that the 'wages for housework' campaign, as a political outcome of this politicisation of the household, whilst bringing to the fore the socially productive aspect of a form of labour that capital appropriates for 'free' (albeit via the intermediary of the wage), as a natural good and as an extension of the 'free use' of natural

---

[11] Leopoldina Fortunati, *The Arcane of Reproduction*, New York: Autonomedia, 1995.

resources, is simultaneously engaged in the would-be measure of these 'non material use values', these aspects of labour with an emotional content. Whilst such measure could reduce the room for manoeuvre, cutting out the margin for species-activity for-itself (becoming), the explicit valorisation of affective labour (traditionally seen as women's work) in such places as the social welfare sector etc, have gathered such a pace that, who knows, the gap between the forms of labour in the productive and reproductive sectors has been drastically reduced. This is not a theme that was ever taken up by the Workers' Movement in any way other than as a marginal or supplementary form (cf. the role of women in the Miners' Strike). It may, furthermore, be an outcome of the discrediting of utopian movements and experiments in collective living as being somehow a 'bohemian withdrawal' that removed the conceptual framework through which the affective component of reproductive labour and the affective component, as energy, of traditional manufacturing labour could have been brought into a conjunction that made both forms of labour a matter of an immanent affective classes?

The stakes of this unacknowledged reproductive labour, a labour that has been invisible, is such that Colette Guillaumin, writing in 1978, has spoken of a 'pre-emption of labour power' that takes a form through which 'we can detect a material appropriation of the body.'[12] This appropriation is, for Guillaumin, premised on women being 'common property' in a patriarchal society; a common that is used unsparingly like any other 'natural resource'. But what is appropriated, at least traditionally from women, is the labour power of child-rearing that is responsible for nothing less than the development of human beings, the reproduction of the species (what greater

---

12 Colette Guillaumin, 'The Practice of Power and Belief in Nature' in *Sex In Question – French Materialist Feminism*, D. Leonard and L. Adkins (Eds.), London: Taylor and Adkins, 1996.

affective task is there?) We are perhaps back with Adler and his 'underlying affective state' in that bringing up children is a work not only of tending to material needs, but to enigmatic, pre-verbalisable affective needs that go towards our developing as desiring beings, as suffering beings and hence as passionately energetic beings. What does such a 'labour' in the home entail?

Adopting an orthodox Freudian approach is enough to start with: the home is the place where instincts are gradually tempered to become socially acceptable, where desire finds its modulation and its ever present surplus (of energy); it is in the home where a sublimation of sexual energies, a changing of the path of the drive, is first come across as a rise in concentration rather than a continuation of a polymorphous, diffuse desire (but always maintaining the embedded diffusion of desire as an unconscious aim); it is the home in which there is a certain internalisation of the mode of being and loving of the adult world (experienced as a 'seduction' which is in itself a means of forming drive-energy, i.e. meaning is constructed from interpreting 'instinctual pressures'); likewise, it is in the home in which the internal responsibilisation (guilt) towards the demands of a 'super-ego' figure or castigating parent is first experienced (hence the energy for conformity in that 'failure to do' incurs some random punishment cf. Kafka); it is the home in which language is inhabited, played with and harnessed first as a sensual oral experience and then as a frustrating (and thus energising) lack of fit between feeling and expression; it is in the home that initial identities are formed from the parental mirror and the encounter with the, at first, well negotiated 'other'; an 'other' the encounter with which is itself energising (with the energy of the desire for the desire of the other... as friend, as lover, as colleague, as collaborator etc.); it is, crucially, from the 'secure base' of the home that the first steps are taken into a wider world of experience and social engagement (where energy is generated from identifications that construct a sense of self as 'ego precipitates'). So, this foregoing thumbnail appraisal of what can be at stake in reproductive labour comes to light as a species-activity in that meeting the sum total of human needs that are presented by infants is a matter of a labour power become 'bios'.

Another important and perhaps neglected aspect of this reproduction of the species, the process of 'growing up' is, as Donald Winnicott would have it, concerned with a move from absolute dependence (upon the parents) towards a never quite achieved independence (we are never socially alone and self-reliant).[13] This is itself a factor in the formation of our energies and its inhibition: remaining, as some males like my grandfather did, utterly dependent for their reproductive needs upon their wives, leads to a reactivation of the 'absolute dependence' upon their mothers; an unconscious affect felt as residual shame and as a compulsion to expiate that I believe made my grandfather, at times, a cantankerous workaholic and, at times, a brutal father (beating a son who reminded him of his own state of absolute dependence?) This drive for independence is one of the means by which capital harnesses labour power as a mythic self-reliance, as a passion for self-preservation and it is, after all, the objective of domestic labour: to prepare the child for the world of work. Fending for ourselves, moving towards independence, becomes for Winnicott, a marker of the transition from the pleasure principle to the reality principle, but the reality of capital makes this transition deeply disturbing and the resultant adolescent conflicts come to be an indicator of the deep affective contradictions that rend 'domestic labour'.

So, in tracing a little the dynamics of 'reproductive labour' which is as much about the production of harnessable energy as the production of subjects, we can see that one of the sources of Marx's labour power is perhaps not simply a physical

---

13 Donald Winnicott, *The Maturational Process and the Facilitating Environment*, London: Karnac, 1990, p.46.

refuelling every night, but a life of layered affective experiences that are often held in a fragile equilibrium. This very fragility, emotional precarity and its dependence upon others, could be said to be a marker of our inability to 'master affect' once and for all for we cannot master the fact that we are embroiled (from uterus to family and beyond) in an intermeshing of affective communication that instils this energy (or exhaustion) in us. But this fragility is, as Fortunati points out, also a chance to evade the control of capitalistic determinations and maybe more. This 'more' may well entail, when affect is recognised as an inter-relational formation that is not sought to be denied by subjects being defined as well-boundaried individuals, an active resistance to its valorisation. Just as Julia Kristeva speaks of a mother's drives as not being inhibited 'but deflected onto another rather than an object' [14], it is a resistance that profiles species-activity as producing 'non material use values' by means of 'free labour'. But when these very immaterial affects of being human and 'working on' the other are brought into the current of valorisation (made into objects) the resultant transformation of them as 'abstract labour' (in the post-Fordist work process) is felt as the acute pain of dehumanisation. In other words the qualitative timelessness for caring labour becomes subject to a socially enforced average time slot (abstract time) that removes 'living attention' and empathy. The bereaved is left crying as we take away the signed document.

---

14 Julia Kristeva: *Kristeva Live*, London: Continuum, 2005, p.70.

4. The Becomings of Capital: The Production of Despair

> The intense and prolonged investment of mental and libidinal energies in the labour process has created conditions of psychic collapse
>
> – Franco 'Bifo' Berardi[15]

(i) Man/Machine

The real subsumption of life under capitalism attempts to remove suffering by dehumanising us. Wielding our sensitivity and aggression in order to get paid we instrumentalise the species-being in more ways than just physical exertion. We instrumentalise to the point of cynicism, to the point of not being able to feel for or feel with. Nothing is worth caring about except the final vial of morphine. This is the dystopian vision in which it seems capitalist modes of life have, with open arms, colonised the species-being. Just as Leopoldina Forunati speaks of women as machines of domestic labour and Mariarosa Dalla Costa of the colonisation of the uterus, so too, this tendency was encapsulated by Adorno when he used the phrase 'organic composition of man'. For Adorno the sale of labour power is an *a priori* given (formal subsumption). What this saleability gives rise to is the auto-transformation of the living into 'a thing, equipment'.[16] Real subsumption, starkly phrased by Adorno, as 'self-preservation forfeiting itself', can be creative of sadistic subjects and much work comes to involve a form of cruelty, a dispassionateness, as we are urged to 'fight our own corner' and to 'not take it home with us'. This lack of feeling,

---

15 Franco 'Bifo' Berardi, *Precarious Rhapsody*, New York: ‹∴MinOr∴›C0mp0siti0ns, 2009.

16 Theodor Adorno, *Minima Moralia*, London: Verso, 1999, p.230.

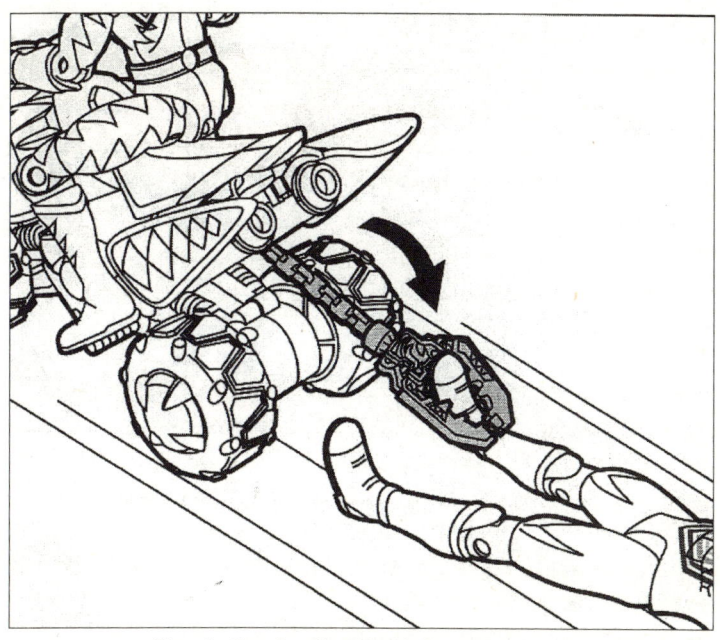

'How to Use Grapling Hook', Power Rangers,
BVS Entertainment, 2003

lack of contact with the potential of the species-being, this professional cynicism is indicative of our imbrication within the *dispositifs* (apparatuses) that determine our behaviour at work. The machines that regulate the pace, direction and aim of work (be they equipment or written work instructions) end up making will-less machines of us. As Boltanski and Chiapello point out, 'product standardisation is applied to persons.'[17] We are overdetermined by functions that divorce us from thought and even further remove us from feeling.

On a less literal footing, the man/machine coupling comes to effect a depletion of the potentialities of the species-being just

---

17   Luc Boltanski and Eve Chiapello, *The New Spirit of Capitalism*, London: Verso, 2005, p.465.

as capital seeks to explicitly harness these by means of affective labour and the notion of work as vocational self-fulfilment, self-appreciation (human capital). The progressive division of labour that amounts to a de-skilling of work is felt as a kind of emptiness and purposelessness in the worker. Work tasks are broken down into 'abstract' minuscule actions that can be performed almost without thinking. Similarly, communicative skills are broken down into corporate slogans and set-texts to be read-out parrot fashion. This 'fractalisation' of the work experience both makes it easier to manage-measure the work process and sorely foreshortens any autonomy or slack that can be generated by 'living labour'. The great hopes of the proletarian revolution were rather based upon a notion of labour power as concrete labour, as a living labour that could liberate us from the value imperative. What has instead occurred is, as Moishe Postone has pointed out, that 'abstract labour begins to quantify and shape concrete labour in its image; the abstract domination of value begins to be materialised in the labour process itself.'[18] The materialisation of value in the labour process takes the form of its fractalisation, the intense measurement of labour in relation to targets, the intense accounting in relation to materials and the intense timing in relation to globalised logistic chains. The removal of the means of production from the species means that there is no longer any unmediated personal interaction, but instead, by way of abstract labour, there is an 'objectified social mediation' (value) that puts us at several steps removed both from subsistence goods, services and the labouring experience of each other. That much new work depends upon the fractalisation of work processes by means of sub-contracting

---

18 Moishe Postone, *Time, Labour and Social Domination*, Cambridge: Cambridge University Press, 1996, p.182. For a text that tries to get to grips with Postone's complex work and that parallels to a degree this current effort see my 'Toward Agonism', 2006, http://www.metamute.org/en/toward-agonism

or the incidence of new 'toll gates' in once 'whole' production circuits, goes some way to remove people even further from the chance of unmediated personal contact. So, with wage labour as the main activity of life under capitalism, our experience of the social and of others is mediated by the 'impersonal objective necessity' of having to work and, say, having to use automated (im)personal services. The lack of choice extends to the lack of choice as to whom we buy from and with whom we work and by extension an estranging element of the impersonal enters into our relational life. This lack of choice instilled by the value imperative of capital ('objectified abstract labour') is felt as a 'non conscious social determination', an obsessive compulsion to work, a pleasure in self-preservation.

Postone expands this idea of the value-form as a determinant of social life from its position in the labour process out to social life as a whole: 'the category of value, as the basic category of capitalist relations of production, is also the initial determination of alienated social structures.'[19] With labour as a pivotal social form in capital (and, as abstract labour, profiling how labour mediates and manages itself) it is offered that the social mediations that ensue are productive not only of goods, but of social relations that themselves are objectified and made abstract. What is instaurated in this way, by 'a social function of labour', are forms of institution and procedures that 'rule' over the society as a whole. In effect the worker produces, by means of this socially mediating form of labour, 'an abstract structure of social domination' that formally went under the name of God. This has many parallels. For Althusser it is what he calls the 'society effect', for Foucault it is the *'dispositif'* or 'apparatus' and for Deleuze and Guattari it is the 'abstract machine'. What these all amount to is the intensification of social mediation. Postone: 'Social domination in capitalism does

---

19   Ibid., p.159.

not, at its most fundamental level, consist in the domination of people by other people, but in the domination of people by abstract social structures that people themselves constitute.'[20] So, a ramification of this could be that 'social domination' has become the aim of production – the '*dispositifs*', mechanisms of control and means of the production of subjects, proliferate to the extent that philosopher Giorgio Agamben feels able to redraw antagonistic class relations into an agonistic opposition between 'living beings (substance)' and 'apparatus in which living beings are increasingly captured.'[21] This is not such a far cry from the would-be notion of the affective classes.

(ii) Entrepreneuriat

One of the mainstays of Marxist theory is the concept of 'reification'. That in a system of generalised exchange, where one worker is exchangeable for another, where the worker as 'man-machine' becomes an object indistinguishable from a commodity object (worth less in some cases), where relationships can be usurious as each figures as a switch point for the valorisation of capital, its continued circulation; in these circumstances it is only a small step towards feeling at home in an entrepreneurial form that has accompanied the ongoing rise of financialisation. One could say, too, that the long domestic process of 'training the drives', of socialising them, is, in fact, relaxed by the entrepreneurial form: there is a suspension of repression as the drive to accumulate, exploit and be cruel can be given free reign. The drive-energy that needs to be tempered when dealing attentively with another can be unleashed with impunity when the other figures as an object, be it worker,

---

20   Ibid., p.30.
21   Giorgio Agamben, *What Is An Apparatus?*, Stanford: Stanford University Press, 2009, p.13.

supplier, customer etc. In a society geared towards and actively promoting the entrepreneurial form ('socialisation of business risks'[22]) this impunity is guaranteed something like 'diplomatic immunity'. There is very little need for conscience or to have forethought for another when a full-on narcissism is not only provoked but rewarded and fêted. So, Foucault's description of the Ordoliberals and their reconstruction plan for an 'enterprise society' in post-war Germany not only highlights the aim of the 'multiplication of the enterprise form in a social body [...] making it the formative power of society', but also the increased urge to commodify that which formerly escaped commodification, such as affect.[23] As Boltanski and Chiapello remark, this line between 'profit and morality' has become seriously blurred as the increasing depiction of labour power as the personal possession of skills 'attributes a directly economic value to persons' that makes workers into entrepreneurs without an enterprise.[24] It increases a sense of 'self-interest' (rather than the disinterest of 'non-material use values') which is the precondition to embrace the entrepreneurial form as a way of being liberated from wage labour. When this is coupled to a change in the nature of work from a contractual relation that leaves some slack for autonomy into work as a means of pleasureable 'self-fulfilment', then all our energies become directed to labouring for self in a manner that would befit a super-ego authored contract.

The turning away from wage labour becomes not a 'refusal of work' but a further cause for the investment of desire in work *per se*: an intensive workload that is not that far removed from

---

[22] See Federico Chicci's 'On the Threshold of Capital, at the Threshold of the Common', in Andrea Fumagalli and Sandro Mezzadra (Ed.) *Crisis in the Global Economy: Financial Markets, Social Struggles, and New Political Scenarios*, Los Angeles: Semiotext(e), 2010, p.43.

[23] Michel Foucault, *The Birth of Biopolitics*, Basingstoke: Palgrave Macmillan, 2008, p.148.

[24] Boltanski and Chiapello, op. cit., p.465.

the labour of reproducing the species which is similarly seen as vocational and a matter of 'self-fulfilment'. The entrepreneurial form as the perverted form of 'desiring production' that, having a quotient of self-interest, becomes an extension of the production of subjectivity under the value imperative: the entrepreneurial is encouraged (the 1980s Enterprise Allowance scheme, tax breaks, subsidies), and thus produces the person as an entrepreneur. The enterprise is made to seem desirable as the dominant subjective form rather than necessary for survival, just as the family, as the 'first economic unit', was necessary for survival. So, reading out from Fortunati there is maybe a further factor in this entrepreneurial desire of the worker as she maintains that the payment for housework (as a portion of the wage) figures the working class male (or wage earner) as a 'representative of capital'. She says that, historically, the man 'buys the woman's labour power with his wage' and that his wage is seen as a 'variable capital' which, she has it, can 'function as capital within [the sphere of] reproduction.'[25]

Does this all this add up to a further departure of the working class to a capitalist heaven? Is it not here too, between the lines, that Adorno can speak of the worker as an 'agent of the law of value'? He is valued as labour power, as fixed capital, and in the home, as the purchaser of labour and as the dispenser of wages; as a switchpoint in the circulation of value. He functions as the capitalist of the household and as Foucault puts it, echoing the theorists of human capital, he has a 'capital-ability' that makes him appear 'as a sort of enterprise for himself'.[26] Likewise, the rise of credit over the past 20 years has entrepreneurial ramifications in that one of the elements of entrepreneurialism is 'raising capital'. Whilst credit has been used to counterbalance the decrease in wages there is an element to credit that takes

---

25 Leopoldina Fortunati, op. cit.
26 Foucault, op cit, p.225.

us beyond that of its being a wage supplement. Namely our becoming accustomed to the 'capital-ability' of credit, breaking the taboo of being in the red. Just as the entrepreneurial form is extended to society so too, then, is the access to credit similarly rolled out. For Marx this has a dramatic consequence: 'in credit, the man himself, instead of metal or paper, has become the mediator of exchange, not however, as a man, but as a mode of existence of capital and interest [...] With the credit relationship, it is not the case that money is abolished in man, but that man himself is turned into money, or money is incorporated in him.'[27] Furthermore, as Bifo Berardi maintains, there has been an ideological identification of labour and enterprise since the 1980s. To be your own boss means not so much that you gain a sense of freedom, but that you fall under the rubric of your own command, a command that is the proxy for a law of value that has 'anthropomorphised'. Deleuze: 'One tells the subject that the more he obeys, the more he commands, since he obeys only himself.'[28]

(iii) Relationship Breakdown

The effects of the rise of abstract labour are manifold and indeed they have already been registered above as, in part, the fractalisation of labour, and the rise of the entrepreneurial form. What can be said about abstract labour is that it represents an increased sense of mediation between human beings that adds up to a growing sense of human powerlessness. At work the job can never be done as it is dependent upon a myriad of other component parts/management ratifications and in

---

[27] Karl Marx cited by Jacques Camatte in 'Capital and Community', http://www.marxists.org/archive/camatte/capcom/index.htm

[28] Gilles Deleuze, *Two Regimes of Madness*, Los Angeles: Semiotext(e), 2006, p.16.

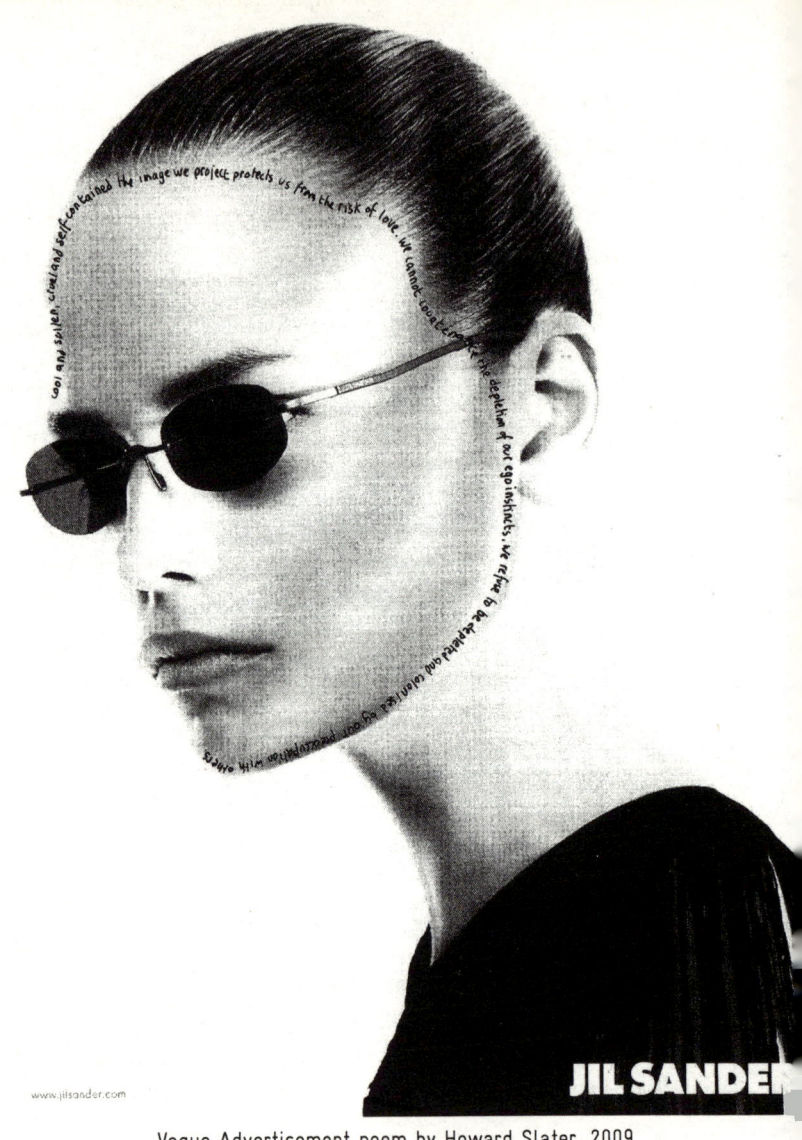

Vogue Advertisement poem by Howard Slater, 2009

the entrepreneurial form we see an increase in small scale enterprises that proliferate mediation and seek to profit from introducing service charges where formally there were none. What this increase in mediation, this growing abstraction of labour, amounts to is a growing estrangement of people from each other at the same time that, contradictorily, there is an increased focus on the very 'material' of relationships in society. This estrangement is complicated, made schizophrenic, by the fact that as Postone maintains, social life under capitalism is experienced as 'personal independence in the framework of a system of objective dependence.'[29] There is supposed to be volitional choice but this is mediated at every turn by the *dispositifs* and 'abstract operative rules' of social institutions, of an instaurated law of value. This in turn gives rise to resentments between people as they experience (or re-experience childhood) dependency that, under capital's increasingly abstract mediations, become reified dependency relations. Marx: 'the reified dependency relation is nothing more than social relations which have become independent and now enter into opposition to the seemingly independent individuals.'[30] We may have here what could be called an extended adolescent conflict with (parental) powers of determination and rule making wherein the children struggle to see the source of the adult power.

So, in opposition to this sense of powerlessness it appears that 'personal independence' is fetishised by the subjects of capital. This would ring true for the entrepreneurial form in that the entrepreneur clings to the idea of his/her personal independence that he/she is in control of circumstances, that there is a sovereign power attending to the person of the entrepreneur. This explains, in part, the desiring appeal of the

---

29 Postone, op. cit., p.125.
30 Karl Marx cited by Jacques Camatte, op. cit.

entrepreneurial form: its denial of reified dependency relations. What's more, and linked to entrepreneurship, 'personal independence' becomes operational through 'self-interest' and the disavowal of dependent relationships. The person hell bent on proving their personal independence gets ample opportunity to fulfil themselves. This can extend from the actual purchase of another person's labour power which makes them dependent on you, to the cultivation of generalised indifference to others, a degrading of any power of empathy. It follows from this that 'pathologies' such as narcissism with their problematising of a desiring relation to the other are deeply imbued within this society and its cultural forms. The 'other' itself becomes the source of new forms of labour that in seeking to regulate social life seek to reduce the possibility of the 'fortuitous' encounter and the establishment of an affective relational-life outside of the grid-work of a socius that seeks to delimit the resonant borders of the 'self' and preserve 'independence'.

Such a desire for the self, as given form by property and ownership, militates against any resonating cohesion in social relationships which, after all, are held together as enforced mediations, as abstractions that are not 'directly lived'. As mediations, as indirect forms of human communication with goals that can be attained by means of people (humans as fixed capital), capitalist social relations do not instil any sense of conscience. Moreover such relations are prone to encourage projection of the worst of ourselves onto convenient objects and thus become the apparatus of a guilt-free self-interest. We need not care what another thinks or feels as long as we can use them as fixed capital and as a depository for the unconscious anger we feel towards our dependent selves. Indeed such projections allow for a renewed sense of our own mythic independence, they demarcate our boundaried 'selves' and, bearing in mind the massive incidence of such projections, go a long way in forming the tenor of many social relationships and social institutions.

(iv) War at the Membrane[31]

One of the key areas of this prolonged myth of 'independent selves' is sensual experience. This is not to deny the positivity of the sensual or affective, but to see how this part of our species-being is harnessed and exploited for the cause of value. Our sensual lives, then, when harnessed as 'pleasure' are seen as an element of self-fulfilment and this in part explains why theories of the transmission of affect get short shrift in that they erode the boundaries of the self-contained subject and profile the interconnectedness of conscious and unconscious mutual dependencies.[32] Pleasure on the other hand – and we can think here of the entertainment industry as well as the repressive desublimation of sexuality – is such that, following the Freudian model, it instils notions of a personalised equilibrium and a sensation centred in a boundaried body. This is the economic efficacy of identities and the blind spot of an identity politics that defies becoming. The 'equilibrium' of pleasure attests to an economicisation or rationalisation of sensuality and its overloading, in the Freudian model, gives rise to a pathologisation in terms of perversion, abnormality and the fear of trauma. The 'boundaried body' too, attests to a problematisation of the relationship to the other and gives rise to a kind of 'war of need' where the other can figure as object. The prevailing profession of street prostitution is central here: a conscience-free using of another's body for personal pleasure that often entails a relational exchange that is minimised in

---

31 For a more protracted take on this notion in which it is discussed in relation to noise and improvised musics see my 'Prisoners of the Earth Come Out! – Notes Towards a War at the Membrane' in *Noise & Capitalism*, Mattin and Anthony Iles (Eds.), San Sebastián: Arteleku Audiolab, 2009, pp.151–165, http://www.arteleku.net/noise_capitalism/

32 Teresa Brennan, *The Transmission of Affect*, New York: Cornell University Press, 2004.

Anomie/Bonhomie: Notes Towards the 'Affective Classes'

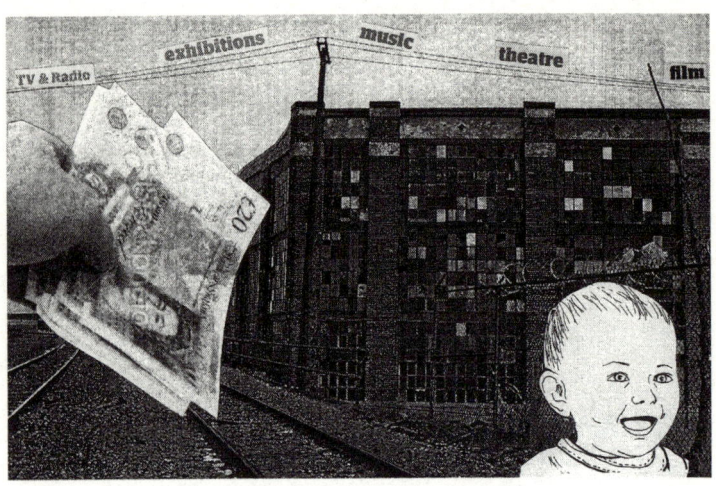

Collage by Howard Slater, 2010

favour of the prostitute's body as a living fixed capital (the other is, in Deleuze's terms, 'separated from the expressivity that constitutes it', and is over-laden with the projective expressivity that another [punter] requires of it). So, there is pleasure as a physical venting, as a projection of fantasy and as a replacement for relational connectedness.

The economicisation of sensuality proceeds in other directions as well. It can well be, like affect, that the sensual is a key facet of the 'vital force' of labour especially as it is harnessed by the 'caring professions' and by the notions of 'added value' and 'going the extra mile'. It can figure as that element of labour that is surplus to its immediate measure as value and that, moreover, represents the ongoing exploitation of human capacities outside the bounds of 'production proper'. As Bifo Berardi maintains 'sensuality is directly invested.'[33] This can mean both the growing sense that work (abstract labour) should be pleasurable

---

33 Franco 'Bifo' Berardi, *Soul at Work*, Los Angeles: Semiotext(e), 2009, p.135.

and fulfilling and in the actual harnessing of human sensual powers as a direct productive factor. Sensuality as labour power. Perhaps the best example of such sensual labour is being raised as the 'attention economy'. All labour requires attention and its correlates such as concentration and a certain investment of desire. Attention, too, figures as 'focus' and 'commitment' and, it is hoped, as pleasure and sensual gratification. The rise of all-pervasive audio-visual technologies from photography to cinema to TV to computers have figured as means of production and reproduction of entertainment and control. They have figured as means of industrialising sensuality. Jonathan Crary speaks of how capitalist modernity has 'generated a constant re-creation of the conditions of sensory experience – a revolutionising of the means of perception.'[34] A facet of this extension of perception is that visual representations come to take on a key role in the increasing mediation that results from the rise of 'abstract labour'; the mediations themselves cry out for our attention and, as such, are increasingly programmed to elicit sensual responses.

Another commentator, Jonathan Beller, has gone as far as to suggest that it is now possible to speak of an 'attention theory of value': 'As a capitalised fragment, that is, as a form of production for exchange, the image will introduce a new dimension to our old category "labour", shifting labour itself toward the province of mediation.' For Beller, the cinematic image is a dematerialised form of the commodity that 'extracts sensual labour (attention)

---

34 Jonathan Crary, *Suspension of Perception*, Cambridge: MIT Press, 2000, p.13. He writes, 'the attentive subject is part of an internalisation of discipline imperatives', p.73. For Antonio Negri, the attention economy is described as 'the interest/will to include in economic calculations the interactivity of the user of communication services.' See his 'Value and Affect', www.generation-online.org/t/valueaffect.htm

directly in the moment of its apprehension.'[35] The instantaneous circulation of the image leads to an intensification of sensual labour in that the time between perception and comprehension is limited. Processing time is foreshortened in a reduction of the human to the speeds of fixed capital. Bifo Berardi acknowledges this as an asymmetry between the format of emission – the audio visual – and the format of reception – the human body, which leads to exhaustion and psychic collapse. Attention, as a 'live' mode of processing perception, is expected, under these productive conditions, to present itself as 'reified attention', as productive information. Could it be said, then, that our senses, as these inform our powers of attention (sensual labour), are the last vestige of our potential autonomy from the valorising effect of value? As Georg Franck wrote 'attention is the essence of being conscious' and if consciousness is dependent on sensory perception then, the real subsumption of labour requires that the whole human being be valorised.[36] The sensual membrane becomes the conflictual threshold to the mobile factory of the sensorium.

(v) Production of Subjectivity

The valorisation of our 'conscious being' is tantamount to the production of the human subject under the mediating direction of the abstract operative rules of a *dispositif*-ridden capital. Is this not what Foucault was examining when he wrote his genealogies of madness, the clinic, the prison, discourse, neoliberalism etc? The production of subjects by means of multiform apparatuses

---

35   Jonathan Beller, 'Vertov and the Film of Money', *Boundary 2*, 26.3, 1999, pp.151-199, http://muse.jhu.edu/journals/boundary/v026/26.3beller.html

36   Georg Franck, 'The Economy of Attention', http://www.heise.de/tp/r4/artikel/5/5567/1.html

that form a reiterative and interpolative habitat; that form, in Camatte's parlance, the 'material community of capital'? In a succinct summation Bifo Berardi offers such biopolitical moves as representing 'a morphogenic modeling of the living operated by the habitat with which it is required to interact.'[37] That this can link the biopolitical turn of real subsumption to the production of subjectivity is maybe not new, but what it points to could well be informed by the 'decomposition' of the working class as a viable social actor. In the case that the working class has been recomposed to heaven there appears a void in the social system whereby the working class refuses its own reproduction as working class (refuses to take pleasure in its own self-preservation struggle). There is a crisis of the reproduction of the working class that once provided a state of equilibrium. From this, then, there arises a necessity to have control of and a direct input into the production of the subject so as to ensure the reproduction of the social system.

Henri Lefebvre, as one of the first Marx-informed thinkers to focus his attention on 'everyday life', seemed to do so by offering as its corollary that the production of the relations of production (capitalist social relations) was coming to supersede those of the reproduction of the means of production. In other words, and akin to Foucault, he asserted that 'there is no re-production of social relations without a certain production of those relations.'[38] The subject comes to be the site of a production that ensures the reproduction of the value-form (as it is personified in individuals). Key for Lefebvre, as part of this social reproduction, is the maintenance and constant reproducing of 'relations of dependence' and, whilst he does not link this directly to the value-form, we can add that this dependence is perhaps what

---

37 Berardi, The Soul at Work, op. cit., p.187.
38 Henri Lefebvre, *The Survival of Capitalism*, London: Allison & Busby, 1978, p.11.

is produced and reiterated by the constant rise of mediation and brokerage, of disciplinary boundaries and the psychic compartmentalism that are instituted by the predominance of abstract labour. Debord's spectacle-effect articulates this in the realm of images but there is also, as Lefebvre also points out, the mediating effects as they are exercised in the 'interior of each individual': the ego is said to command the id and the super-ego exercises dominance over the ego.[39] Here, we can rejoin domestic labour and perhaps see that it is here that 'the real development of the individual' begins. In the domestic sphere it is said to be about the natural dependence of the infant that elicits a 'living attention' (Brennan) from the parent, but in the wider social reproductive sphere it could well be about an artificially prolonged dependence (necessary for the production of value) that elicits a harnessing of 'selective attention'. This latter too could feed into the means by which perception is guided away from a recognition of the multiple mediations that surround the subject and is fed, once more, into the myth of independence. Repression is non-originary but an effect of the law of value that brokers someone else's desire to us at half the price.

It could be that the crisis in what constitutes 'production proper' is also compelling an increased accent upon the production of subjects that translates into their being permeated by the value-form; not only becoming fixed capital and 'independent centres of circulation'[40], but in having their desire mediated by 'repressing representations'. The real subsumption of labour figures as the increasing 'abstract domination of value' (Postone) over people as it is coupled to subjectivising institutions: the mediation between people that constitute value (value as representation) finds its institutional expression

---

39 Ibid, p.87.
40 Marx, op. cit., p.419.

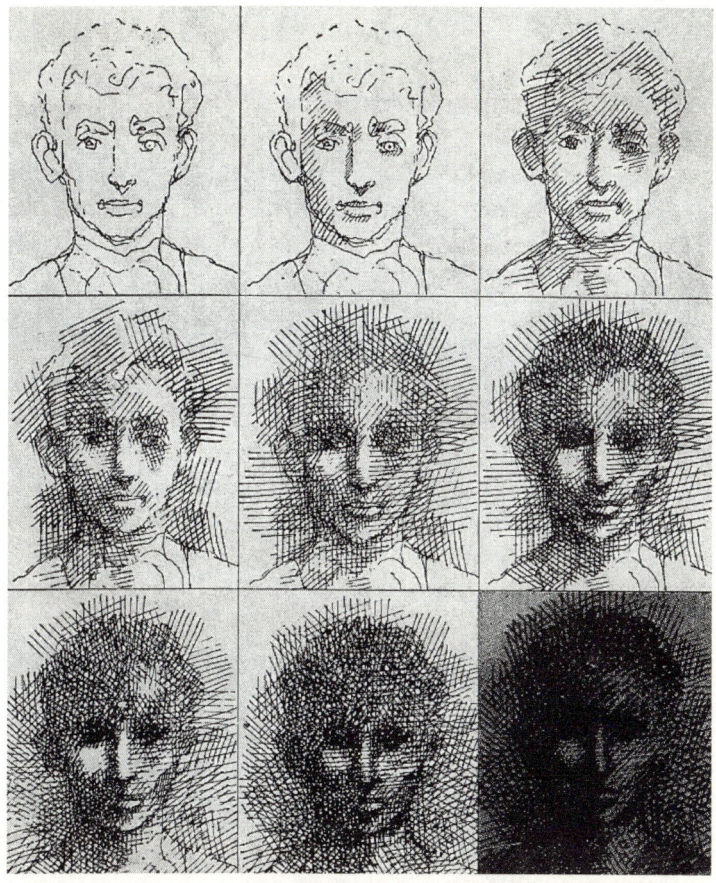

Adapted from the cover of *Pierre: Or, The Ambiguities*, Herman Melville, Signet, 1964

in 'abstract operative rules' (value as command). In some senses the 'source of value' has, with the lengthening of the working day into a lifetime, moved away from any strict measure, but the tools of production too have been transformed (computation) as has the 'vital force' required to animate production (sensuality, language, affect). This could even extend to the process of production itself which becomes a matter of recombination or transduction (the creation of objects from already extent components); a kind of production from the already produced that, in the guise of 'a history alienated no longer' Postone maintains could lead to a new concept of production divorced from abstract labour and its correlate, abstract time.

This dimly extrapolated alternative highlights a divergence between production for 'social wealth' and production for 'value'. That the latter permeates this society may account for why social therapist Lois Holzman has maintained that the 'world's people have stopped developing' and that the 'contemporary self' is 'an impediment to human developing and learning.'[41] This impediment may well be an outcome of the renewed production of subjectivity as one receptive to the value-form and hence receptive and unconcerned by the increasing compartmentalisation of life experiences. A compartmentalisation that Agamben has recently maintained is one of the main functions of *dispositifs*: desire must be kept in separate spheres, as independent from the desires of others. Thus the 'production of desire' as a means of reproducing the attractive pole of the *dispositif* ('the drive in the institution') rather than a nonconformist 'desiring production' that is open to the propulsive and differentiating desire of others. In this way desires, as a component in the production of subjectivity, are made malleable and predisposed to an authorititative injunction to desire within the framework of the *dispositif*. Holzman and co-writer Newman can thus speak of 'the human capacity to authoritarianly commodify' ourselves which maybe hinges on the fear of losing all desire and the threat of

---

41 Lois Holzhomn, 'How Much of a Loss is the Loss of the Self', http://loisholzman.org/publications-articles-chapters-and-manuscripts. Writing in 1948 André Breton would have concurred: 'The species that seemed to be on the way to definite stagnation/incapable of a renewed creeping life.' See his *Ode to Charles Fourier*, London: Cape, 1969.

disintegration that this perhaps implies.⁴² This extends to a reluctance to express 'malfunctions'. Modelled on 'fixed capital' the man/machine, unlike HAL, cannot break down or show even a chink in the ability to go on. When emotionality is expressed is it not, amidst the prevailing competitiveness, seen as a sign of weakness? Does it not expose itself to the risk of exposing its vulnerability? For Holzman, perhaps in full appraisal of the value-form permeating the species-being, the resultant psychic pain reveals itself in people coming to see themselves as 'non-human objects'.

This is one inhuman turn that Bifo's 'morphogenic modeling of the living' can take and behind this lies the very real effect of capital's subsumption-production of the subject in that drive-formation, by means of the introjection of others' projections and societal injunctions, is such that instincts/drives become entrained along predetermined 'pathways'. This is perhaps the full effect of the 'production of the subject' in that pre-produced aims for the drives are fully prepared to be cathected by means of social institutions and forms such as entrepreneurial culture, the myth of independence etc. When Deleuze and Guattari mention, in passing, the 'drive in the institution' they are perhaps hinting at such a 'morphogenic modelling', in that desiring-perception is actively attracted to the protective benefits of such institutions as work and university, the family and the spectacle. Klossowski: 'the language of institutions has taken over this body, moreover taken over what is "functional" in my body for

---

42 Lois Holzman and Fred Newman,. 'Power, Authority and Pointless Activity', in T. Strong and D. Paré (Eds.), *Furthering Talk: Advances in the Discursive Therapies,* Kluwer Academic/Plenum, 2004, pp.73-86, http://loisholzman.org/publications-articles-chapters-and-manuscripts/

the best preservation of the species.'[43] The seeking after self-preservation in the best interest of each individual member of a species is the way that an anthropormorphised capital attracts drives to its front organisations; institutions like those of the Worker's Movement that promise an alleviation of suffering and, consequently, a mastering of affect. For a group analyst like R.D. Hinshelwood it is institutions that can 'provide an internal support to an individual's own defence mechanisms.'[44] The exchange here is, once more, the offer of independence within the confines of a dependence that amounts to a passion for function, for defensive self-preservation only.

5. Mogadon Capital

> I live beneath a political tyranny which, although it does not oppress me directly, still offends some hidden principle of my soul
> – Fernando Pessoa [45]

There are many definitions of depression. The foregoing thumbnail depictions of some of the 'becomings' of capital and the way they effect us could join the definitions: being

---

[43] Pierre Klossowski, *Sade, My Neighbour*, London: Quartet, 1992, p.36. On this see also Klaus Theweleit: 'It is a feature of some institutions that they dictate specific ways on making object choices.' See his *Object-Choice*, London: Verso, 1994, p.31.

[44] R.D. Hinshelwood, *What Happens in Groups*, London: Free Association Books, 1987, p.71. Hinshelwood talks of institutions as 'social defence systems' and 'collective defences' that, in part, offer defence against unpleasant experiences and maintain roles that restrict potential becomings – both of these are elements in self-preservation, in preserving the self from the 'unknown I-state' that can arise in the group experience.

[45] Fernando Pessoa, *The Book Of Disquiet*, London: Serpents Tail, 1991, p.69.

overdetermined and will-less, dependent and compelled beyond our ken whilst being urged to the maximum self-fulfilment and independence is a 'schizophrenisation' too far for many. The intensities of a labour that demand improvisation, language skills, professionalised affect and a suspension of empathy do not reap such benefits as to allow us the luxury of coping with existential anxieties and the species-suffering of ourselves as sensual and passionate beings. The manifold mediations of social life, growing social phobias and the competitive accent of self-promotion assist in divorcing us from forms of relational life that could be non-judgemental, empathic and congruent; in other words provide the minimum from which we can regain confidence and become human. The solution offered seems to be an entrepreneurial insensitivity from which many do not awaken, nor can afford to awaken. That such social anguish is being remarked upon is no surprise but, as usual, its being noticed is dependent upon welfare cash costs. Patrick Butler, reporting on a recent dossier by the Young Foundation, paraphrases that 'millions of people are unhappy, lonely and unable to cope with profound changes in the workplace.' Quoting the dossier itself he reports: 'a more overtly meritocratic society has encouraged people to be more ambitious for themselves, but also made them more vulnerable to failures – and more likely to blame themselves (rather than fate or the class system) if things go wrong.'[46] The picture painted is one of job insecurity, socialised vulnerability and emotional precarity held together in a fragile affective equilibrium. The fallout of the recent 'credit crunch' as it wends its cutting way through local services is only exacerbating this subsuming effect of the value-form as its circulation instils and diffuses depression and hopelessness:

---

46 Patrick Butler, 'Millions of Britons Unhappy', *The Guardian*, 7 February 2009.

CITALOPRAM 10, 20 & 40 mg
FILM-COATED TABLETS

PACKAGE LEAFLET: INFORMATION FOR THE USER

Read all of this leaflet carefully before you start taking this medicine.
- Keep this leaflet. You may need to read it again.
- If you have further questions, please ask your doctor or pharmacist.
- This medicine has been prescribed for you. Do not pass it on to others, it may harm them, even if their symptoms are the same as yours.
- If any of the side effects get serious, or if you notice any side effects not listed in this leaflet, please tell your doctor or pharmacist.

IN THIS LEAFLET

1. What Citalopram is and what it is used for
2. Before you take Citalopram
3. How to take Citalopram
4. Possible side effects
5. How to store Citalopram
6. Further information

1. WHAT CITALOPRAM IS AND WHAT IT IS USED FOR

- Citalopram belongs to a group of antidepressants known as selective serotonin reuptake inhibitors (SSRIs).
- Citalopram is used for the treatment of depression (major depressive episodes).

2. BEFORE YOU TAKE CITALOPRAM

Do NOT take Citalopram:
- If you are allergic (hypersensitive) to citalopram or any of the other ingredients of this medicine
- If you are taking, or have taken in the last 2 weeks a antidepressant medicine of the type called mono ___ inhibitors (MAOIs) e.g. selegiline or moclobem___

Take special care with Citalopram:
- Use in children and adolescents under 1___ Citalopram should normally not be use___ adolescents under 18 years. Also, you ___ patients under 18 have an increased r___ as suicide attempt, suicidal thoughts an___ aggression, oppositional behaviour a___ take this class of medicines. Despite th___ prescribe Citalopram for patients und___ decides that this is in their best interest___ prescribed Citalopram for a patient und___ discuss this, going back to your doctor___ your doctor if any of the symptoms listed a___ worsen when patients under 18 are taking C___ the long-term safety effects concerning growt___ and cognitive and behavioural development of Citalo___ age group have not yet been demonstrated.

Tell your doctor or pharmacist before you start to take this medicine if you:
- Have thoughts of suicide or self harm. Occasionally, these thoughts may occur or increase in the first few weeks of treatment for depression, until the antidepressant effect becomes apparent. Tell your doctor immediately if you have any distressing thoughts or experiences.
- Suffer from diabetes, treatment with Citalopram may alter control of your sugar levels
- Suffer from epilepsy or seizures, as seizures are a potential risk with antidepressant drugs
- Receive electro-convulsive therapy
- Have history of mania/hypomania, citalopram should be used with caution and should be discontinued when you enter a manic phase
- Have kidney or liver problems
- Have a bleeding disorder, Citalopram may cause bleeding
- Are using medicinal products that affect the clotting of blood
- Have a stomach ulcer or have had any bleeding in the stomach or intestine in the past
- Suffer from irregular heartbeat/palpitations or any other heart proble___ s (if you are susceptible to QT-inte___ al prolongation or have s___ spected congeni___ l long QT-syndr___ me)
- Suffer ___ om low blood p___ assium or mag___ sium levels
- Suffer ___ om psychosis w___ h depressive ep___ odes
- Experi___ ce 'serotonin sy___ rome.' A combi___ tion of symptom___ such ___ gitation, trem___ muscle contrac___ ns and ___ la may indic___ e the developm___ t of this condit___ ___ b Citalop___ should be di___ inued immedia___ ___ stop___ withdrawal s___ oms may occur ___ op___ italopram)

- Other medicinal prod___ ___ serotonergic effects such as oxitriptan, other tript___ ___ phan
- An anticoagulant (to ___ ood clotting), e.g. warfar___ aspirin (acetylsalicylic ___ ___ idamole or ticlo___
- Herbal preparations ___ St John's wort (___ perforatum)
- Pain-relief ___ es calle___ anti-inflam___ ketoprofen___
- Medicine___
- Medicine___ fluvoxa___ antidep___
- Medicin___ tripta___
- Medicin___ propafe___
- Medicines ___
- Medicines fo___ ___ or chlorpromazine
- Medicines for stom___ ___ prazole or cimetidine

Please tell your doctor or ___ ___ or have recently taken any other m___ ___ es obtained without a prescription.

Taking Citalopram with f___
You are advised not to d___ ___ l whilst taking Citalopram. Citalopram can be take___ ___ thout food.

Pregnancy
There is only limited experience concerning the use of Citalopram during pregnancy. Do not take Citalopram if you are pregnant or planning to become pregnant, unless your doctor considers it absolutely necessary.
You should not discontinue treatment with Citalopram abruptly. If you are taking Citalopram in the last 3 months of pregnancy, let your doctor know as your baby might have some symptoms when it is born. These symptoms usually begin during the first 24 hours after the baby is born. They include not being able to sleep or feed ___, trouble with breathing, a blue-ish skin or being too hot ___ ng sick, crying a lot, stiff or floppy muscles, lethargy, ___ or firs. If your baby has any of these symptoms ___ ontact your doctor who will be able to advise you. ___ pharmacist for advice before taking any

___ breast milk in small amounts. There is a ___ baby. If you are taking Citalopram, talk to ___ start breast-feeding.
___ macist for advice before taking any medicine.

___ chines
___ t your ability to drive a car or use machines.
___ machines until you know how Citalopram ___ e ask your doctor or pharmacist if you are ___ nything.

___ nt information about some of the ingredients of Citalopram
This medicinal product contains lactose. If you have been told by your doctor that you have an intolerance to some sugars, contact your doctor before taking this medicinal product.

3. HOW TO TAKE CITALOPRAM

Always take Citalopram exactly as your doctor has told you. You should check with your doctor or pharmacist if you are not sure. Citalopram should be taken as a single dose, either in the morning or the evening. The tablets can be taken with or without food. The tablets should be swallowed with a drink of water or other fluid. Citalopram does not work immediately. Usually, an effect will be felt after 3-4 weeks. Treatment should continue until you are free of symptoms for 4-6 months. Citalopram should be withdrawn slowly. It is advised that the dose is gradually reduced over a 1-2 week period. Do not stop taking Citalopram even if you begin to feel better, unless you are told to do so by the doctor. Never change the dose of your medicine without talking to your doctor first.

The usual dose is:

Adults
The recomm___ nded starting d___ se is 20 mg per ___ y. If neces___ ry ___ the dose c___ be increased u___ to 40 mg per da___ depending ___ h ___ response. T___ maximum do___ is 60 mg p___ da___

Elderly pa___ ents (>65 ___ ar of age)
For elderly ___ tients the ___ se should be re___ ed to half of t___ adults, e.g. ___ -20 mg pe___ ___ ay. Depending ___ the individual response o___ he patient, ___ ose can be ___ eased. The ma___ m ___ dose fo___ patients ___ 4 ___ g per day.

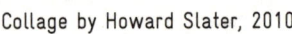

Collage by Howard Slater, 2010

> The number of antidepressants prescribed by the NHS has almost doubled in the last decade, and rose sharply last year as the recession bit [...] The Health Service issued 39.1m prescriptions for drugs to tackle depression in England in 2009, compared with 20.1m in 1999 – a 95 percent jump.[47]

However, it is not only charitable foundations, professional journals and government sponsored think tanks that are taking notice of these issues. Scattered throughout the pronouncement of the insurrectionary Greeks of 2008 were such phrases as 'the middle and lower classes are exhausted' and 'we are shaking with worry over the future of our children'. A World Revolution manifesto from the same period included amongst its appellants 'the clinically depressed'. In the popular booklet, *The Coming Insurrection,* it was offered movingly that 'society is run on a gigantic reservoir of unwept tears'. In a joint declaration of an Argentinian 'Network of Alternative Resistance' from 1999, it is offered that sadness is the 'way in which capitalism is present in our lives'. There is, then, a renewed awareness of, as Bifo puts it, the question of sensibility becoming one with politics. In his re-reading of Guattari, Bifo has recently drawn attention to capital as a 'pathogenic mechanism' and, perhaps as a means to cathect suffering, has called for an 'awareness of depression that would not be depressing'. Taking up Felix Guattari's call for 'personal problems' to be able to 'irrupt on the private or public scene of ecosophic enunciation', Bifo has proposed that future political action is endangered lest it include 'modalities of therapeutic intervention [...] to reweave the fabric of social relations.'[48] How could social relations be reweaved? Could

---

47 'Antidepressant use rises' in Therapy Today, Vol. 21/Issue 6, July 2010.
48 Felix Guattari, *Chaosmosis*, Sydney: Power Publications, 1995, p.128; Franco 'Bifo' Berardi, op. cit., p.134.

this 'therapeutic intervention' be the task of an affective class? Julia Kristeva saw this as a possibility to create a political space from the foundation up, from experiences of encountering one another rather than from discursive proxy-enunciations cut off from experience. Drawing on her experience as an analyst she wrote that 'freedom consists in revealing yourself to the other [...] we experience our similarities and incompatibilities and in revealing them, we reveal ourselves and that's how we become.'[49]

This kind of psycho-politics has had a long and foiled history that stretches at least as far back as Reich's Sexpol movement and the rise of group psychotherapy and up through feminist 'consciousness raising' groups, encounter groups and anti-psychiatric ventures such as Villa 21, Kingsley Hall and the therapeutic communities associated with The Philadelphia Association (which is not to forget cultural movements from Artaud to Mad Pride and the Asylum collective in the UK). What makes it different in our times is that the growing endocolonisation (including the governmental regularisation of the up-to-now confidential and potentially autonomous space of therapeutic counselling) can extend to an 'inner dialogue' that, having continually to ingurgitate the ever changing 'abstract operative rules', exercises a debilitating 'conditionality' over us that is less benign than a negotiable 'super-ego'. Depression can be a paralysis, a refraction, a self-blame that is rarely recognised as a suffering under a 'political tyranny', but as a personal and personalised failing. This endocolonialisation, the progressive exploitation of the non-material use values of 'species-life', is having an endemic impact on mental health to the degree that the former Labour Government appointed LSE professor Lord Layard as a 'Happiness Czar'. It was also planning to have cognitive behavioural therapists installed in UK job centres.

---

49 Julia Kristeva, *Revolt She Said*, Los Angeles: Semiotext(e), 2002, p.76.

Other statistics are always coming to light such as that reported by Allegra Stratton: 'Some 6 million adults in the UK have been diagnosed with depression or anxiety,'[50] This can translate into a suicide rate, especially amongst young men, that is said to be rising, and there was, in 2007, the grim outbreak of what the media called a 'suicide cult' in the former industrial hub of Bridgend. 'Hidden principles' (made up, for me, from an other-centred sensuous practice) are being more than 'offended'. They are being permanently occluded by a socially produced 'arrested development' that could find its conceptual twin in Postone's notion of capital's 'treadmill effect'.

What is also disturbing is the effect of the Left's 'disenchantment' with itself, with its subject etc. This has led to the quest for a new social subject (Negri and Hardt's multitude, Bifo's cognitariat etc), a questioning of modes of organisation and new theoretical tools ('communisation', 'capital as subject', 'value-form theory' etc). Unfortunately, this very disenchantment, while discernible in a constant reiteration of 'truths' and a self-certainty that itself could be deemed pathological, is very reluctant to bring itself to expression. One factor in depression is the hardening and clogging up of the self-image, there is an immovability that is the inverse of a 'becoming' and an opening out to new experiences. The problem of the other is guarded against. It is too risky to adopt experimental positions in a reception context that expects the same 'litany' and in fact retroactively instils the 'litany' as a factor in belonging. You are who you are. An identity is won and this is a struggle in itself. An identity as a first step towards independence, but then there arises a dependency on this

---

50 Allegra Stratton, 'Unemployed to be offered "talking treatment"', *The Guardian*, 5 December 2009. Darian Leader is less empirically minded: 'The more that society insists on the values of efficiency and economic productivity, the more depression will proliferate as a necessary consequence.' See *The New Black*, London: Penguin, 2008, p.13.

identity and hence our 'litanies' harden; we become identifiable and attractive of a 'living attention' which we do not want to lose. This could well be a description of all forms of social-relational life from infancy through adolescent and so on. It could well be speaking of our 'reputation' at work or amidst 'comrades' etc. But does this not amount to the way our refrains and institutions, in a manner akin to abstract labour, 'organise stabilities for our dependencies'[51] which are themselves the source of a constant psychic struggle? This foregoing may be a description of 'defensiveness', a mechanism of self-maintenance that is intimately tied-in to the reproduction of social relations. For the Left, with its advocated concern for the other sufferer, there is a taboo on its own suffering which disables it from speaking of its own disenchantment, an abreaction of which, a 'speaking of depression in a non depressive way', could well bring forth the relief of acknowledged sadness and the exploration of feelings that subsist within us that are not readily articulateable but which may well reveal the 'becomings' that capital has made of us. As Marx had it: we must get beyond the 'stage of self-reference in alienation.'[52]

6. Hidden Affects

> Society exists in part through invisible transmission
> – Francis Picabia[53]

All is not lost. Depression and anxiety are forms of communication. Some could say they are forms of protest.

---

51   Anon, *Call*, (n.d.), p.80.
52   Marx, op. cit., p.398.
53   Francis Picabia, *I am a Beautiful Monster,* Cambridge: MIT Press, 2007.

Something is retaliating, something is happening at a level that is outside our consciousness, our vocabulary, but which we have perceived, been affected by. Something that feels, at first, unspeakable. A feeling of being possessed. The body is semioticising to us and if we listen we may hear the ingurgitated conditions of worth from the super-ego of an identitarian, culpabalising, obsessiveness-inducing value-form known as capital. Just listening to the 'non-negotiable threat' of this all pervasive and purblind 'subject' may well be to dissipate the horror we feel for the bogeymen we cannot see and who never reveal themselves. But how do we open negotiations? Writer Teresa Brennan may well have responded that we open negotiations by no longer being resistant to the idea that our 'emotions are not altogether our own', by coming to acknowledge the 'invisible transmission' of socially-induced affect and its effect upon our mode of self-relating as modulated by the value-form. This would coincide with a notion of affect as 'pre-personal' and as preceding the subjectivising forces of will and consciousness and their interpellation. We can feel an atmosphere in a room, a sensation in our body, an intuition that is difficult to express. We cannot assign these a source and have the traumatic experience that our sense of self is no longer bounded but porous. Teresa Brennan, hinting at the difficulties of delineating the differences between affect, feeling and emotion, has it that feelings are 'sensations that have found the right match in words'. Eric Shouse, drawing upon the work of Brian Massumi, concurs when he states that feeling is a 'sensation that has been checked against previous sensations and labelled', it has found a word-representative. An emotion, for Shouse, is 'the projection/display of a feeling' and affect 'is unformed and unstructured (abstract).'[54] Returning to Walter Benjamin, this maybe adds extra weight to his contention that an affect cannot be mastered, it can be 'discerned' as Brennan would say, and this would be to acknowledge the force of affect as a kind of 'radical alterity'.

Before taking up some of these dimensions and with lip service to the notion of affect as a 'vital force' informing the notions of labour power, it may be useful to speak, as Marx does of labour, of a two-fold depiction of affect. There is concrete affect as emotion and feeling that is seen as informing a 'feminisation of labour' and there is abstract affect as 'invisible transmission'. On the one hand a 'living attention' that mobilises the senses and is the being as that which can be affected, moved and other-orientated. Here there is a certain amount of discernment or consciousness attached to affect. Its 'feminine' depiction, then, is linked back to reproductive labour, or, if we take Irigaray's suggestion that woman is closest to a mediation capacity, it is a work that has as its object the reproduction of social relations. This speculative notion of 'concrete affect' as concrete labour finds its foiled category in the notion of 'affective labour' which more or less serves the purpose of putting more 'living' into 'living labour'. On the other hand, then, with 'abstract affect' we have a being which could be said to be overdetermined or subject to influences which it cannot control and struggles to name. The lack of 'discernment' informed by the fear of being porous and dependent here leads to the defensive strategy of projection to ward off our experience of affect as a threatening alterity. Brennan: 'one is sealed off by the projective-affective transfers that purchase the sense of self containment' or 'a projection is

---

54 Eric Shouse, 'Feeling, Emotion, Affect', *M/C Journal,* Vol.8, Issue 6, December 2005, http://journal.media-culture.org.au/0512/03-shouse.php. The easy delineation of these may run into difficulties when we come to attempt to 'discern' the affect. An affect may be experimented with as a feeling yet the word may not be 'right' etc.

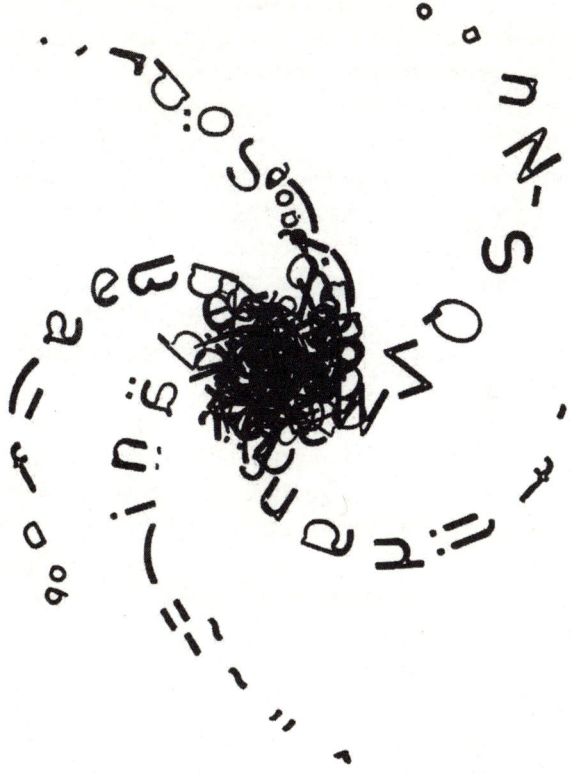

Concrete Poem by Neil Mills from 'And 5', 1969

what I disown in myself and see in you.'[55] Here with an 'abstract labour' of affect we may get an inkling of the production of capitalist social relations that Postone was investigating. Unconscious affect and its projective dynamic could also be productive of 'non conscious social determinations'. Something indecipherable that escapes from consciousness, that is pre-personal, but which exercises an influence or effect upon us.

---

55 Teresa Brennan, op. cit., p.114.

Anomie/Bonhomie: Notes Towards the 'Affective Classes'

Into this dense network of projection that figures as the social creation of an 'abstract labour' of affect we have the libidinal inflection of a primary narcissism bolstered by the presuppositions of the value-form: i.e. private property re-instils a sense of the 'reduced other' and informs the affect of jealousy which in turn informs paranoia. An absolute dependence on the multiple mediations of society triggers the contemporaneous infantile layer of dependence upon parents which in turn triggers, when faced with the 'abstract operative rules' of these mediations, a sense both of impotence (which leads to independent, monadic rage) and a disavowed dependency on others (which puts pressure on us as 'individual identities' as well as forming within our social-us a lack of confidence.) This misfiring social relation informed by the value-form is also related to a 'personal protectionism'. Teresa Brennan developed an idea called the 'foundational phantasy' through which this personal protectionism is seen as the pre-individual source of misfiring non-communication: we judge the other (beginning with mother) as the source of unwanted affect within us and in turn project out. André Green: 'But one is amazed how many of the deaf dialogues are about the non-perception of the most common affects either in oneself or in the other.'[56] Maybe André Green should not have been so amazed. Aren't these 'deaf dialogues' the consequence of the will to independence? Are they not intimately tied to maintaining performance levels? Are they not elements of repression? Do they not fall foul of a fear of 'radical alterity', of an inability to discern those very pre-personal affects that open us out to a thrilling abeyance; an abeyance that in its 'othering' forecloses the polymorphous sensual in foreclosing our approach of the other.

---

56 André Green, *The Fabric of Affect*, London: Routledge, 1996, p.284.

7. Distributed Vulnerabilities

> It would be [...] incumbent upon us to listen, within ourselves, scornful of that critical spirit, to grasp our physiologically most concealed voices
> – René Ménil[57]

To some degree the value-form is creative of 'reified dependency relations' that being experienced ubiquitously are experienced by all. A facet of this is the projection, or 'othering', of disowned affective elements of ourselves onto others who figure for us as 'objects'. This self-protective dynamic, informed by a will to alleviate its suffering and master affect, would then include a disavowal of our 'sensuous being' and its capacity to feel, a reduction of passion and an occlusion of dependency itself in favour of the upholding of an 'aimed for' and valorisable independence. In some senses this projective dynamic, fearful of unavoidable vulnerabilities, seeks to sidestep the social itself and disinvests human interconnectedness and hence the species-being. Wilfred Bion has it that 'the individual is a group animal at war, not simply with the group, but with himself for being a group animal and with those aspects of his personality that constitutes his 'groupishness.'[58] This 'group animal' aspect could well be taken to mean the various configurations of a self as they are informed and modulated by indiscernible affective

---

57 René Ménil in *Reflections of The Shadow – Surrealism and the Caribbean*, Michael Richardson (Ed.), London: Verso, 1996, p.131.
58 W.R. Bion, *Experiences in Groups,* London: Tavistock, 1985, p.131. Another early group-therapy practitioner, Trigant Burrow, writing in 1950, spoke of a 'restricted behavioural personality', an 'autopathy', which he called the 'I-persona' through which 'each constituted himself as the centre of motivation, and each thus became the sole and absolute authority in respect to human conduct.', http://www.lifwynnfoundation.org/trigant.htm

resonances, but the individual's being 'at war with the group' is an indication of the repressing of any notion of dependency which may reveal beneath it a reluctance to suffer the rupture of a self-image through immersion in a group experience that, in its transmission of affects, marks a passage to an 'unknown-I state' (a pre-personal singularity); an experience prior to or beyond that of 'self-reference in alienation'. As Judith Butler maintains, our existence as social beings implies just such an ontological vulnerability, just such a haphazard abeyance, in that 'our life is always in the hands of others' to the degree that she maintains the body itself is a 'social phenomenon'. We are affectively exposed to others and, she says, 'vulnerable by definition.'[59]

One could say, then, that we are made even more vulnerable by our reluctance to express our vulnerability and this reluctance, aside from the socially induced passion for self-preservation, lies in that schizophrenising aspect of capitalist social relations that measures each against each whilst at the same time proffering a similitude that makes each exchangeable for the other. This has the effect of instaurating a judgemental conditionality, a policing of the other and of difference that may well rise from our own internalising of meretricious judgement by means of comparing ourselves to others. Is the aim of all this competitiveness to become 'general equivalents' as people? That Benjamin didn't advocate a 'mastery of affect' could further suggest that the way was left open for us to distribute vulnerabilities, communicate them, in an exploration of our dependencies. This could well reveal how 'affect is never merely our own: affect is [...] communicated from elsewhere. It disposes us to perceive the world in a certain way, to let certain dimensions of the world in and to resist others.'[60] This

---

59 Judith Butler, op. cit.
60 Ibid.

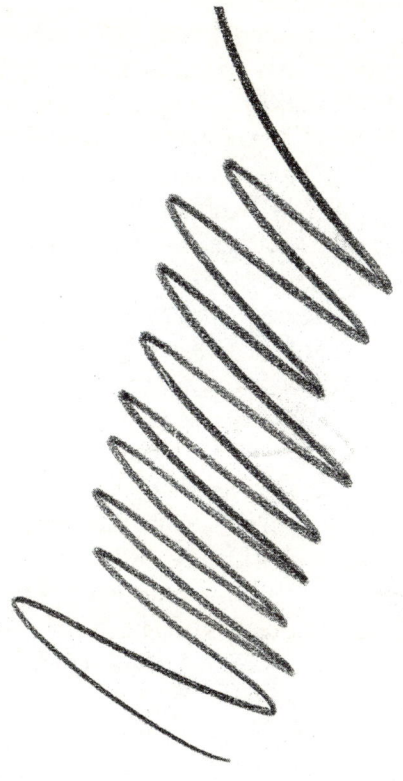

Drawing by Howard Slater, 2010

chimes with Brennan's notion of 'discernment' and could lead to giving affect its properly social dimension, transforming it into an unregulated social force in the moment of its straining towards articulation. The distribution of vulnerabilities, then, would come up against the forms by which it is 'differentially allocated' (the full range of socially induced vulnerabilities and precariousness) as well as how it is regulated ('made other' or, as much feminist literature has offered, 'made pathological').

In this light Bifo Berardi's call, following Guattari and indeed the Women's Liberation Movement, for future political action to include 'modalities of therapeutic intervention [...] to reweave the fabric of social relations' could be tantamount to a 'distribution of vulnerabilities'. The statistics quoted earlier show a social fabric that is ringed with depression, hopelessness and the exodus of internal-exile. Any left wing resurgence would be a non-starter if the people it was trying to reach lack the confidence to leave the house let alone come to some discerning means-of-expression and articulation of their sorrow. Even deeper than this, the obsessive compulsive disorder induced by the value-form, is creating automated somnambulant and 'generally equivalent' subjects. As noted above, the left is in a state of disenchantment and is still suffering a hangover from the 1980s. It seems powerless to effect and spread some revivified form since the working class went to heaven. The last thing it seems to want to engage in is self-invented forms of therapy that would shift it away from its 'empirical coordinates' into the messy hell of an emotional life that, if distributed in a context of 'affective discernment', could well reveal 'reified dependency relations' (cf. *dispositifs*) and the 'radical alterity' (the singular irreducibility of each rather than their value-driven equivalence) that lies beyond. This hangover of unspoken disenchantment makes it unwelcoming to the 'sick' (or to those just coming to a fledgling self-consciousness of their own 'alienation') and that it doesn't 'distribute its own vulnerabilities' has the effect of replicating the judgemental and regulatory space of capitalist social relations.

All in all it may be necessary to get beyond the 'stage of self-reference in alienation' which could well mean, for the left, a move beyond the alienation of labour towards a recognition, under real subsumption, of the alienation of the species. What's more, this phrase of Marx's could be read, if it were to be practiced, as a therapeutic 'distribution of vulnerabilities' by means of embracing our alienation. Moving from a stage of 'self-reference' may mean we move from a stage of relating to our alienating symptom as a facet of our 'independence' which, in turn, suggests a personal protectionism. It could be that the common therapeutic effect of sharing a vulnerability with other(s) and discovering that others share the same vulnerability is a means of moving on from this stage of 'self reference'. This in itself takes us towards species-being and if this alienation is 'sensually re-appropriated', actualised rather than kept hidden and repressed, if it is allowed to be expressed as fully as possible by means of the body, then our vulnerabilities are distributed as 'non material use values' to others in a mutual quest to become human. Such a distribution of vulnerability (which can, on the whole, be seen as a main tenet of poetry, theatre and music) helps to create solidarities in that the deeply imbued 'independence' within ourselves – that extends to reticence, a fear of being judged and a judging of others – is met with a revelation of our own defensive practice of 'othering' as being a factor in the repression of our own articulation at the same time that our fear of the other is abated and with it the fear of what Pasolini has called 'threatening alterity'. Affective transmission, when discerned and felt in this way, can profile our dependencies to us without feelings of shame. It is not shameful to be subjectified by *dispositifs* and the implied willlessness of this, the overdetermining of a power over us, needs to be faced: 'to go from potentiality to act one must first traverse the impotentiality of our lives, eliminating it fear by fear.'[61]

---

61 Q. Libet, *Pre-occupied – The Logic of Occupation*, printed by the Inoperative Committee, 2009, p.7.

8. Towards The Affective Classes

> because neither are feelings sufficient in an act of balance nor are arguments enough when placed before protocols
> – Nanos Valaoritis[62]

So, with the 'discernment of affect' and the 'distribution of vulnerabilities' we are getting very close to a practice of an affective class that seeks not so much to take over the means of production as reappropriate the means of the production of subjectivity. To re-cap, this immanent class may well have been present as labour power in the classical sense – the energy of production denied a sensibility. It was more visibly present in the domestic labour of the reproduction of the species through which labour power can now be more readily profiled as the 'bios'. Here the issue of 'wages for housework' etc. set a limit point to the valorisation of 'non material use values' as well as profiling a major missed opportunity for the Workers' Movement to revivify itself around the 'suffering species'. The developments in capital which amount to a growing endocolonisation have resulted in forms of sensual labour being deployed that valorise the very senses to the point that it is not just energy that is required from us as labour power but our sensibilities across the duration of a lifetime. This incursion of the value-form makes itself felt as a distance and separation from each other as well as from our own other and, as projective disavowal of the affective fragility we feel, goes towards some indication of what can be meant by 'capitalist social relations'. Underpinning all this is the existential drama of species-life in which suffering is in dialectical relation with sensuousness and this gives rise to a conjunction between the forces of capital and

---

[62] Nanos Valaoritis, *My Afterlife Guaranteed*, San Francisco: City Lights, 1990, p.39.

the historical Worker's Movement: the eradication of suffering (i) by means of instilling a passion for self-preservation (concrete labour) and (ii) the insistent foreclosure of 'living beings' in all their singular alterity by the continual production of *dispositifs* or apparatuses of capture (abstract labour). This readily brings to mind Agamben's re-drawing of the class polarity of worker vs. capital and his concluding offer that 'the restitution to common use of what has been captured' [our very emotional life] 'cannot be properly raised as long as those who are concerned with it are unable to intervene in their own processes of subjectification.' That this chimes with those pronouncements of Berardi, Guattari, Kristeva et al. for a therapeutic politics, is an added mark of urgency for what is at stake for the immanent class of the affective: a process of disidentification which entails the sharing of vulnerabilities, the sensual reappropriation of alienation and the forging of new vectors of social desire.

This implies, once again, something of a break with the models and modes of struggle of the classical Workers' Movement. The old demarcation of mass vs. individual, the baneful repression of any affect not motivated by the 'studious exercise of animosity', may well be being outflanked by the notion of singularities and a collective-psyche in each 'self' which could arise from any discernment of affect and its concomitant making visible of subject-producing *dispositifs*. This is in a sense the 'therapeutic' aspect of the affective classes, an aspect long since scorned as an indulgent and individualist direction by a meretricious left that seems less able to communicate the more its theoretical production proliferates. Berardi has Guattari express the therapeutic in the following way:

> Overcoming depression implies some simple [sic] steps: the deterritorialisation of the obsessive refrain [i.e. *dispositifs*], the refocalisation and change of the landscape of desire [i.e. social need to express 'fragility'], but also the creation of a new constellation of shared

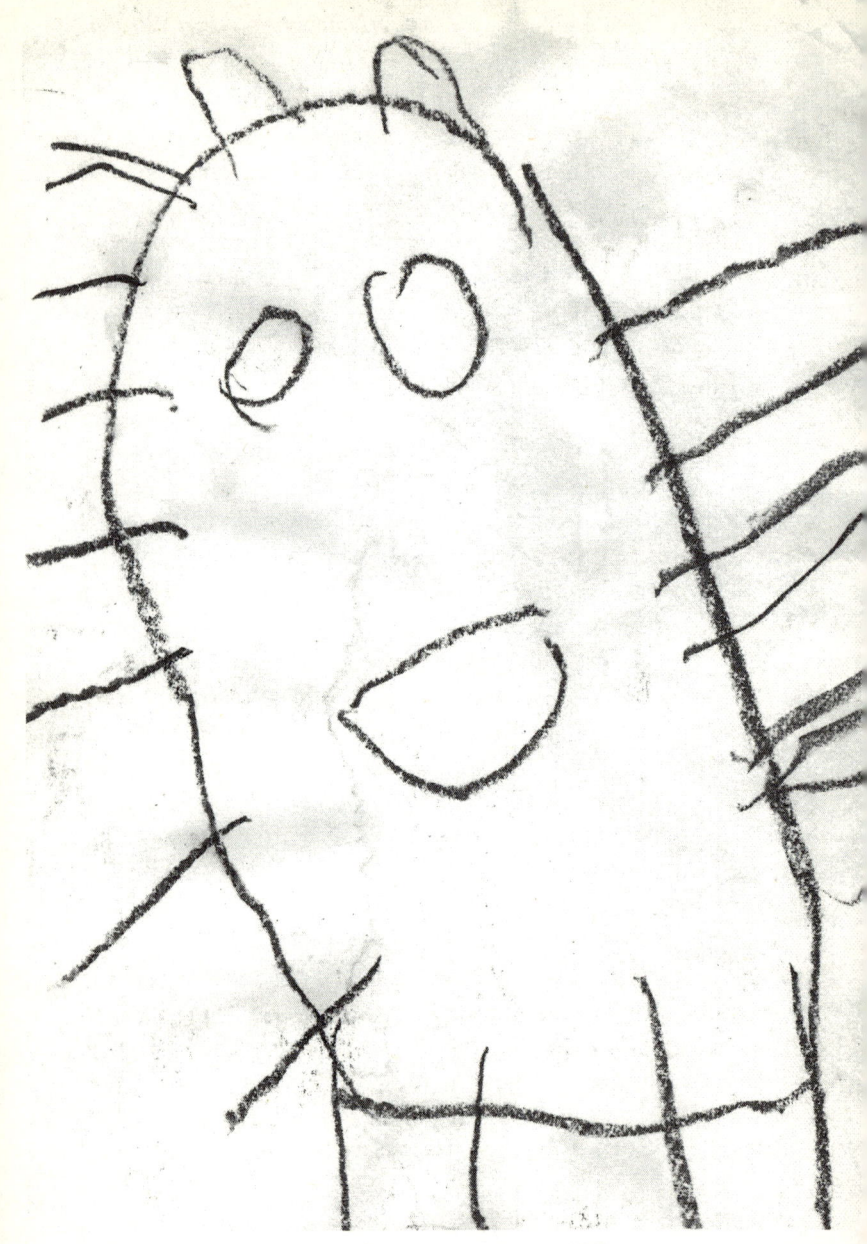

Drawing by Agnes Slater, 2006

beliefs [i.e. immanence of affective class], the common perception of a new psychological environment [i.e. the value-form's endocolonial move] and the construction of new model of relationship [i.e. the avowal of vulnerabilities that militate against reducing ourselves to objects of projection].[63]

In many ways this turn, this therapeutic accent, is suggestive of bringing 'bare life' into communication. If 'bare life' is that which is created from the bios by the multiple action of projection-carrying *dispositifs*, if 'bare life' is the material for the production of subjectivity then this bare life (be it pre-expressive affect that is in dialectical struggle with the *dispositif* of language) should maybe be the re-won 'material' of the affective classes in their quest to get back behind the 'stage of self reference in alienation'. That 'bare life' is mute, unexpressed, not a viable political 'material' is one further reason for a break with the mores of the Workers' Movement as these slowly play themselves out in a nitpicking rhetoricising of strength.

This has obvious problems for a left that has steadily sought to propagandise its strengths rather than its weaknesses. There is nothing more abhorrent to it, nothing more revealing of its tight control of an 'image of opposition', than the taboo on the weak profiling their weakness, becoming 'victims'. Whether this tight control is staged by a 'machismo' or an 'evaluative judgementalism' or an untroubled relationship to language, it all has the same effect: an occlusion of the expression of suffering, a reinforcement of the public/private segregation required of 'working subjects', a defamation of this 'subject' as denied 'bare life', but allotted a 'human' role in one of the multiple *dispositifs*. Solidarity is expected as an emanation of some innate class consciousness rather than as something to be built, renewed. But, as if speaking for the affective classes, Suely

---

63 Berardi, The Soul at Work, op. cit., p.217.

Anomie/Bonhomie: Notes Towards the 'Affective Classes'

Rolnik has written of the anaesthesia of our vulnerabilities to the other, adding

> but vulnerability is the precondition for the other to cease being a simple object for the projection of pre-established images, in order to become a living presence, with whom we can construct the territories of our existence and the changing contours of our subjectivity.[64]

The discomforts that such a collective 'going fragile' can bring are not at all as straightforward as being simply 'hippy' or 'self-indulgent'. These discomforts of communicating from the position of bare life, of a 'produced subject', of trying to surmount the proffered pleasure of self-preservation, of feeling that acute dependency on others, is the necessary pre-condition for the 'becoming of the relation' that is a would-be task of the affective class. What is profiled by such a 'dense atmosphere', common to group psychotherapy, is a kind of 'deterritorialising turbulence' (Rolnik), a 'letting go' in which we can begin not only to discern affects within us and as they circulate between us, but can also come to discern, work with and trace our own projections. As Luce Irigaray has put it: 'recognising our own projections, advancing towards what is most veiled in oneself [...] inscribe in our becoming a more differentiated objective, instead of remaining a blind projection of an unrecognised subjective.'[65] The persistence of roles and our positioning within them makes us blind to the irreducible aspects (singularities) of one another and to the fortuitous encounters that the social could offer.

Projections, then, feel like the value-form in a psychical guise. It is as if a detritus of the production process within

---

64 Suely Rolnik, 'The Geopolitics of Pimping', EIPCP, October 2006, http://transform.eipcp.net/transversal/1106/rolnik/en

65 Luce Irigaray, *The Way of Love*, London: Continuum, 2002, p.94.

us needs to be expelled onto another by means of projection: prejudices, thwarted desire and the foiled will-to-independence circulate through the social system, and are literally dumped like toxic waste on others who are eminently reducible by us to a 'role'. This position of the 'blank screen' is deliberately adopted by psychoanalysts in order to make such projections discernible as the 'transference'. What is often profiled in this way is the 'conditions of worth' that have been instilled in us by our capture in *dispositifs* and how these, inflected with the value-form, effect our mode of communicating with others. In terms of the Workers' Movement, where comrades are supposed to have already 'arrived' at some way of being that is anti-capitalist, such an affective space is more or less impossible as it implies a kind of moving, to cite Irigaray, 'behind oneself constituted as same' as other comrades, and hence a breach in solidarity, a revealing betrayal of a 'real self', a self-exile. An immanent affective class would not look for the weak members in this way; a way that projects our own uncertainties of commitment onto others. An affective practice would take heed of the way that conditions of worth, these vulnerabilities of our 'bare life', these psychic costs of endocolonisation, are felt to only be provisionally expressible on condition of not being judged or assessed or measured as one role or another. So, the push and shove, the verbal discursive jousting of left politics, makes it, despite its casualties, less than a 'safe and secure' space to begin to find words, gestures and dramatisations to express the affective vulnerabilities and to learn from the embodied raw capitalist material that subsists within, without and between.

9. Affective Soviets

> production of (an) encounter(s) without subject(s) or
> [...] (an) encounter(s) that produce subject(s)
> – Colectivo Situaciones[66]

From therapeutic communities to a tearful concert without instruments, from zones of proximal development to prostitute collectives, from the self-exiled seeking phantom organisations to the wailing cries of a room full of mourning, from the changing mat full of shit to the coffin full of unfulfilled desires... the affective classes are maybe seeking to form factories of everyday life, ventilated spaces free from the tyranny of originality and unfearful of the repressed content in the clichés that stumblingly express the pig iron of their sensual labour. Escaping the 'major key' as the house of language collapses on them they wilt before a remembrance of the perfectly formed discourse object of a reified and pre-produced speech. They've left it behind. Exchanged it for the groundless ground of 'bare life'. By means of an ever sharpening concentrated listening that's no longer deemed passive (a political technique they learned as much from music as from diploma courses), they stay with the weak which is all of they and sit with the weight of a dense atmosphere as it forms a stone in their stomachs. A stone that could become a jewel as the silence rings out in a group-formed reductionist piece called 'antique light'. Expectation slides into a loss of language, slides into a phrase from somewhere else that can become a prop. At this moment each is auto-traumatising while being held by a silence that respects the last utterance. What's mine? What's yours? What's between-us? Sun Ra speaks:

---

[66] Colectivo Situaciones, 'Something More on Research Militancy: Foonotes on Procedures and (In)Decisions', *Ephemera* (5) 4, 2005, http://www.ephemeraweb.org/journal/5-4/5-4colectivo.pdf

'there's change in the air can you hear the heavy silence there?'[67] And the change comes from holding back for a change, comes from recognising an interjection as potentially a projection, as some cathartic evaluation that elevates an individual to the detriment of an in-forming singularity. What risk instinct?

Or so it goes. This becoming of the relation when there is 'no longer anything of one's own and nothing yet in common'.[68] And just so it should be, so this concentrated listening forms safety. Safety and form, carefully constructed to be against a representation of itself; safe, for a while, from the implicit misunderstandings of it as a therapeutic, an aesthetic, a musical space. It is all and neither. It is a risk. A risk to be put in charge of the tempo of your own risk. A risk to see through a sea of projections. A risk to come to see differences as palpable and approachable and not the cause once again of egoistic ruptures, of dispositifs of social insecurity. A risk to be improvising with nothing but 'bare life'. A risk to reveal how we've been 'purposed'. But it is not ready-made. Aside from some assurances that all can bring that they too will be learning to speak again, that there will be recourse another day and a day after that the next week, that it is a tempo that could be outside 'abstract time' and as such no statement or stutter remains solidified in a printed or recorded form that pinions its utterer to a 'role'. Safety in absolute recourse to revisit it. Safety to become a 'subjective-object' for ourselves, a fetish object for others as our singularity becomes caressable from afar. Safety in being resolutely against representation for a flow, no matter how slow, could only be but resolutely outside a frame-by-frame capture. Fragility could crack the lens. The lens could intimidate like a silent examiner. The captured subject becomes a photogram of a solidified ego.

---

67 Sun Ra and The Myth Science Solar Arkestra, *Antique Blacks*, London: Art Yard, 2010.

68 Luce Irigaray, op. cit., p.168.

Anomie/Bonhomie: Notes Towards the 'Affective Classes'

Let it all hang out. This is not the '60s no longer. Decades of puritanism followed the psychic casualties of the 'night of the long knives' when 'full personal critique' added a tertiary anxiety to the structurelessness that evoked affect to let it hang there unintegrated, undiscerned, unlocatable within the meshwork of 'ouragonisations'. Personalised co-ordinates, unable to 'comprehend difference in itself, the unequal in its self', bring with them the cess of judgement, the power games of politricking wherein the 'bare life' of vulnerability can be the raw material for another's personal power.[69] No. We be the being of the group-being as alone non-being but together. Any 'affective class' there could be could well be to dangerously propose a human identity prior to a social identity, but as its been said of Augusto Boal's theatre of the oppressed: 'to engage in Boal's therapy is to become situated in a space between the individual and the socialised category of all individuals.'[70] These molar categories of class, gender... these socialised categories... to what level do they occlude the very coming-to-be-real existence of the 'social individual', the species-being? To what extent do the social categories and the identities they propose work to hold us back from a full appraisal of ourselves as social beings? To what extent are they 'repressing representations' or 'delimitations'? Is it not that from the outset, at the very beginnings of each life there is the 'relationship with the other', an introjection of the social through the eyes of another, a 'living attention' that makes us 'social individuals'? Is it not that any immanent 'affective class' is proposing, not an asocial basis from which to proceed, but a paring away of the multiple components of a

---

69 Gilles Deleuze, *The Logic of Sense*, New York: Columbia University Press 1990, p.298.

70 Mady Schutzman, 'Brechtian Shamanism' in *Playing Boal – Theatre, Therapy, Activism*, M.Schutzman and J. Cohen-Cruz (Eds.), Abingdon: Routledge, 2004, p.152.

Anomie/Bonhomie & Other Writings

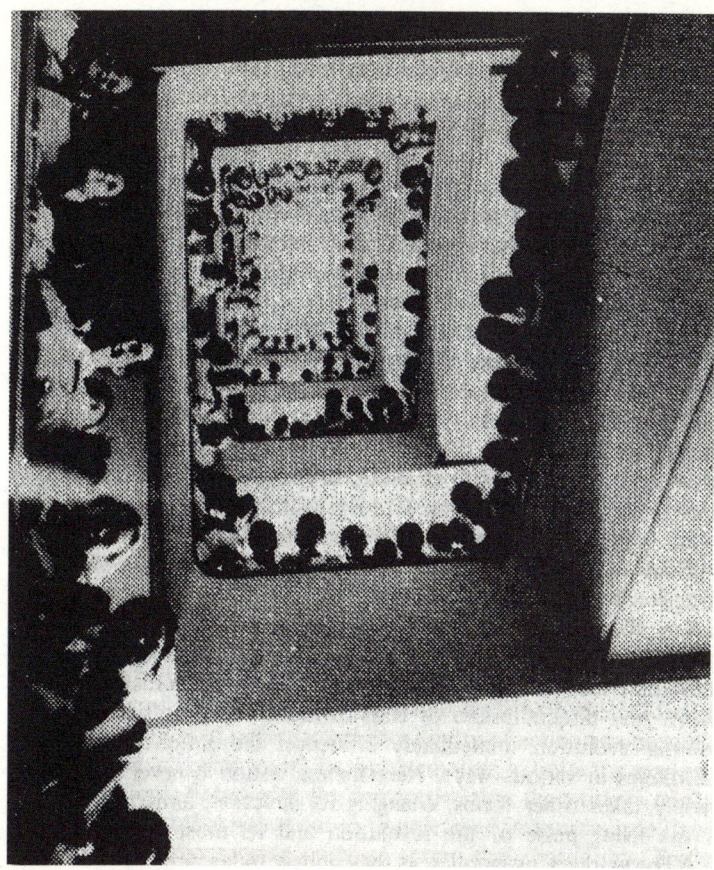

'Lean over the staircase we are going to hold an assembly', from *Wildcat Spain Encounters Democracy*, 1976-1978, BM bis, 1978/79

produced subjectivity to base a common from a molecular and indiscernible scale, the scale of affect? Is it this scale that reveals an ongoing socialisation prior to the categories of capture? As Joan Riviere has put it: 'These other persons are in fact therefore part of ourselves, not indeed the whole of them but such parts or aspects of them that we had our relation with, and as have thus become parts of us [...] We are members one of another.'[71]

But an affective soviet is not ready-made. It's a poetic fantasy. We 'participate in its own enaction', its own lack of proprietorship; for it is collectively produced as an organ for becoming, as a pointlessness past time. That it is a struggle to explain it brings language into relief and our urge to speak is so relieved this way as to be unintentionally 'banal' and 'poetic', to be whatever for a while, to be 'a whatever being, a being such that it is [...] each one of its qualities, adhering to them without allowing any one of them to identify it.'[72] Could these qualities include the opaqueness of affect? 'Adhering' to them in order to explore and discern them? The radical alterity of affect that makes us other to ourselves so we could no longer be subjected by those *dispositifs*, that induced passion for self-preservation, that made us, formerly, to be 'without qualities', without singularity, without encounter, without hope.

All 'eprow' to the affective classes?!

September 2009 – April 2010

---

[71] Joan Riviere, 'The Unconscious Phantasy of an Inner World Reflected in Literature' in *New Directions in Psychoanalysis*, London: Karnac, 1995, pp.358–359.

[72] Giorgio Agamben, *Profanations*, New York: Zone Books, 2007, p.59.

REAL PHÔNÉ[1]

---

[1] Some notes on Jacques Rancière's *Dissensus*, London: Continuum, 2010.

Real Phôné

> it seems that the only thing that counts
> are the words with which all people manifest that
> they wish to stay away from being or action
> – Pierre Guyotat

It seems that one of the original divisions of social life, one which to some degree defines the practice of politics, could well be that which splits off the domestic and reproductive spheres of existence from that of public life. The discriminations that ensue extend to a mode of speech that is permitted into the polis and a mode that, in being akin to animal life, is excluded. Rancière, discussing Aristotle states:

> the sign of the political nature of humans is constituted by their possession of the logos, which is alone able to demonstrate a community in the aesthesis of the just and unjust, in contrast to the *phôné*, appropriate only for expressing feelings of pleasure and displeasure.[2]

In some ways Walter Benjamin's conjectural category of the 'affective classes', a class which would see no regressive wrong in expressing pleasure and displeasure, is one for which *phôné* would be valued and not sought to be converted into *logos* simply in order to be admitted to the polis. If it could be said that the working class was formerly in the position of the excluded and seeking access to representation then the reframing of its anger and suffering into the language of politics has, to a degree, made it a consensual figure. Its visibility by means of representation has made it into a 'figure possessing a specific good or universality' upon which a hoped-for practice is based. Is this maybe why Rancière asserts that 'politics cannot be

---

2 Jacques Rancière, ibid, p.37.

defined on the basis of any pre-existing subject'?[3] For the preexisting subject, one that 'possesses' the *logos*, is already a representation made visible, made perceivable, by the currently operative 'distribution of the sensible' and as such cannot effect a new 'dissensual reconfiguration of the common experience of the sensible'?[4] This may go some way to guessing at Rancière's reasons for the abandonment of class struggle politics, but it does not explicitly explain what 'supplement', what non-existent subject, could come to take its place and effect what could take on a pro-revolutionary hue: the 'redistribution of the sensible'.

It feels like Rancière's notion of the 'distribution of the sensible' is of equal importance for him as such Marxist notions as the 'ownership of the means of production' or the 'redistribution of wealth' are to a more straightforward socialist politics. It seems to figure as a radical concept that may have received its charge back when Rancière was writing about the worker-poets of utopian socialism for whom workers' emancipation was 'not about acquiring a knowledge of their condition it was about configuring a time and space that invalidated the old distribution of the sensible.'[5] It's as if the homogenising effects of capital, its reduction of disposable time and its guiding of the meanders of sensuality, have effected a colonisation of the sensorium, for, by means of what he calls a 'police function', Rancière asserts that this distribution of the sensible 'structures perceptual space in terms of places, functions, aptitudes etc, to the exclusion of any supplement'.[6] One could think here of Deleuze's Control Society ('marketing is now the instrument of social control') or of the effects of the division of labour as they impact upon our ability to sense and

---

3   Ibid., p.28.
4   Ibid., p.140.
5   Jacques Rancière, 'The Emancipated Spectator', *Artforum*, March 2007.
6   Rancière, *Dissensus*, op. cit., p.92.

feel, on the stunting of our experience in favour of the sliced up gridlock of corporate culture. Elsewhere Rancière, more dramatically, has the distribution of the sensible as effecting a 'definite configuration of what is given as our real, as the object of our perceptions and the fields of our interventions.'[7]

Is it maybe in the interests of a self-preservation that this state of affairs is tolerated by many? For what we have with the 'distribution of the sensible' seems to be another more recent police function of preventative measures. The 'distribution of the sensible' protects us from the trauma of unmediated (cultural) experience in order to preserve desire as functional and satisfied with what is already in circulation, to appease our already identified senses (taste). Could one say the 'distribution of the sensible' (carried out not solely by a huge media workforce but by underlying *dispositifs*) is concerned with blocking dissensual interventions by making them imperceivable and hence unconscionable? Erich Fromm certainly thought so when he offered that societies 'develop a system, or categories which determine the form of awareness. This system works, as it were, as a socially conditioned filter.'[8] Is such a 'partitioning', then, a fair distribution according to choice or a structural ruse to avoid the 'common' of shared affect and the rousing of those who 'come to partake in what they have no part in.' Aristotle: 'a lack of strong affection among the ruled is necessary in the interests of obedience and absence of revolt.'[9] This line of enquiry could extend to cultural critics too. The rash of interpretations of objects and oeuvres has not only a publicity outcome but the 'cop in your head' function of prosthetic thought and a reducing of the indeterminacy of chance encounters.

---

7 Ibid., p.148.
8 Erich Fromm cited by Adam Phillips in *On Flirtation*, London: Faber 1994, p.136.
9 Aristotle, *The Politics*, Harmondsworth: Pelican, 1981, p.110.

Where then for the politics of dissensus? Rancière: 'the essence of politics consists in disturbing this arrangement by supplementing it with a part of those without part identified with the community.'[10] But who could this supplement be and from what community? Whilst Rancière offers that this supplement could be made up of those 'with no qualification to rule, which means at once everybody and anyone at all' and whilst this seems less than meretricious, it is still unclear how this 'non-subject' would act to 'redistribute the sensible' (determine for itself the 'form of awareness') or how politics could escape the loop of consensus/dissensus.[11] This is further complicated when Rancière, not picking up again the thread of *phôné* and hence the 'domesticating' sphere, seems to be in accord with a form of civilised consensus when he has it that politics is the 'making of statements and not simply noise'; or, in *On the Shores of Politics*, when he urges individuals to 'tear themselves out of the netherworld of inarticulate sounds.'[12] Taken from the point of view Benjamin's prospective affective class, is it not here, in what is definitively and historically excluded from politics, that the 'non-subject' arises? The rejection of phôné, of the sound of suffering, of noise and its replacement with the functionality of (theoretic and rhetoric) language, is itself a proviso of permanent consensus and a foreclosure of the strong affect needed 'for staging scenes of dissensus'.

In some areas, like music and therapy, noise is a compound of affects; it is that which is not easy to interpret, it is the sound of suffering, of phylogenetic agony, it is the breach of the real as constituted by the *logos*, it is rousing. And as such, as unmediated experience (i.e. non-narrated, non-explicated), as raw nerve,

---

10 Rancière, *Dissensus*, op. cit., p.36.
11 Ibid., p.53.
12 Ibid., p.152; Jacques Rancière, *On the Shores Of Politics*, London: Verso, 2007, p50.

it is neither denounceable, nor decidable nor demonstratable. If this unpolitical sound of suffering, this *phôné*, is difficult to listen to, if it is auto-traumatic, if crucially, it emanates from 'those without part', it could well effect a 'redistribution of the sensible' beyond that of a logos-led dissensus that Rancière asserts is a part and parcel of democracy. A redistribution that could figure the non-subjects as 'whatever singularities' (Giorgio Agamben), as 'approximate people' (René Ménil), as the affective classes through which noise as unnameable affect requests that we attend to it with a non-prosthetic 'living attention'. These non-subjects, then, are those for whom *phôné* can supplant the logos, for whom the convolutions of the diagnosed and the wailings of the infant are communicative. In many ways it is the domestic and reproductive sphere that has never been allotted a 'sensible' and in this light the 'domestic utopia' of Fourier was one attempt at a 'redistribution of the sensible'. Barthes suggests that 'Fourier has chosen domestics over politics' and that his penchant for neologisms 'upsets the laws of language.'[13] With this there seems to be a choice that lies beyond choosing the 'just and the unjust', beyond 'good and evil', in that through the domestic comes the noise of desire and the inconsistent expression of suffering that demands that we hear it with all its lawless and inarticulate *phôné*.

These may be grand claims for a polyvalent noise, but it comes to act as a metaphor for the effects of suffering and the self-exclusion from the polis of those that suffer. Where better to find the 'the interval between identities', that Rancière suggests can found the political subject, than in those 'non-subjects' who in attending to the *phôné* are seeking to refind their species-being through a traumatic refusal of the partitioning effects of identity and the overdetermined forms

---

13 Roland Barthes, *'Fourier' in A Roland Barthes Reader*, London: Vintage, 1993, p.342.

of awareness that this entails.[14] The worker-poets of Rancière's *The Nights of Labour* are said to have 'made themselves "other" in a double hopeless rejection, refusing both to live like workers and to talk like the bourgeoisie.'[15] As workers they were denied access to the 'sensible of poetry', separated from it in a structure of work and militant politics. Being neither workers nor bourgeois puts them in the in-between of a contemporaneous 'distribution of the sensible' (if, in fact, such a distribution allots identities in its operation), and their leaving to found utopian communities was maybe, as with Fourier, their attempt to give their 'redistribution of the sensible' a public space that was not a polis for political subjects but a 'domestic utopia' of approximate people. But what kind of space was this that these worker-poets wanted to create? The practice of poetry, whilst seemingly attributable to the logos, may very well interject too much *phônê* to be taken as political. Is it, then, an Atopic space? When Barthes, in *A Lover's Discourse*, writes of atopia he speaks of 'making language indecisive'. Is he, perhaps, here hinting at a practice of poetry? When he supplements this with 'one cannot speak of the other, about the other [...] the other is unqualifiable' this too sets us at a great distance from the polis for it is there, where the logos reigns, that just these generalising and other-defining modes of speech come to qualify, quantify and speak for the 'supplement' and its anonymous suffering.[16]

Rancière's interest in aesthetics seems to go against what seems to me, in his 'Ten Theses on Politics', to be his pro-political aim of injecting dissensus into the polis to recharge democracy. His fight against consensus in this text seems to be about

---

14   Rancière, *Dissensus*, op. cit., p.56.
15   Jacques Rancière, 'Introduction to Proletarian Nights', Radical Philosophy, No.31, 1982.
16   Roland Barthes, *A Lover's Discourse*, New York: Noonday, 1989, p.35.

saving politics from 'annihilation'.[17] But, if the required modes of 'dissensual subjectification' are such that they should 'reveal a society in its difference to itself' is it not that we have already taken cognisance of this point?[18] The aesthetic discussions that Rancière engages in seems to have much more to start out from in that they allow for and seem to encourage an impact of the aesthetic on the current 'distribution of the sensible'. Art, he suggests can undetermine our awareness, can upset identitarian equilibriums, can introduce us to the forbidden and can encourage our intervention in the 'folds of the real'. Aesthetic practice, then, for me, seems to be charged with revealing the difference in ourselves, with revealing and cultivating a sense of society in ourselves (it could consequently be just as much therapeutic). This troublesome and once pathologisable trait ('we are all a complex of different, miniature groups' – Deleuze), with all its infra-psychic conflicts premising any common transformatory articulation, is a further indication of the relevance of the *phôné* for any 'redistribution of the sensible'.

In his discussion of one of several scenarios for aesthetics, that of 'art becoming life', Rancière has it that for this schema the alternative to politics is 'viewed as the constitution of a new collective ethos.'[19] This view, says Rancière, goes back to Schiller who, it seems, may have had an impact upon the utopians that followed him and whom, Rancière suggests, influenced the young Marx with the synchronous notion of a 'human revolution'. Here communism is seen as the founding of a 'sensory community' that may have more applicability to Fourier's passionate combinations of the phalanstry than the parties and leagues that ensued. And so, what is ushered in by 'sensory community' is the 'affective labour' of domestic and

---

17   Rancière, *Dissensus*, op. cit., p.44.
18   Ibid., p.42.
19   Ibid., p.119.

reproductive work, a *Spieltrieb* or 'play drive', where the relation between non-subjects is neither solely passive nor solely active, that replaces knowing with doing, delegating with sharing, and, who knows, intertwines the partition of the sexes in an imbrication of 'being-there-for' in a shared transitional space.[20]

So, in 'Rethinking the Link', Rancière has it that for Schiller 'the only true revolution would be a revolution overthrowing the power of active understanding over "passive" sensibility, the power of a class of intelligence and activity over a class of sensitivity and wilderness.'[21] One could say that this is not only a restaging of the projected conflict between *logos* and *phôné*, but an indicator that sensitivity and wilderness are the markers of a 'dissensual subjectification', an atopic subjectification that resists its apprehension by a logos-driven normalcy. What could follow from this, then, is a displacement that helps affinities to assemble: 'I divine that the true site of originality and strength is neither the other nor myself, but our relation itself.'[22] The 'class' that Schiller speaks of, then (as well as perhaps hinting at Benjamin's 'affective classes'), is perhaps premised on relational affinity: the unoriginal and thus unifying predisposition to sensual belonging which is a spark for singularities. For Fourier these singularities may well have taken the form of the perversions he encouraged into collective expression. The 'redistribution of the sensible' that such shared perversions could occasion may very well have led to a far-reaching challenge to the 'determined forms of awareness' in that, following Lacan, perversion could well be seen as 'the privileged exploration of

---

20 Ibid., p.116.
21 Jacques Rancière, 'Rethinking the Link', http://www.16beavergroup.org/monday/archives/001881.php
22 Barthes, op. cit., p35.

an existential possibility of human nature.'[23]

However, leaving aside Fourier's ideas for a 'collective prostitution' as well as the 'reciprocal polygamy' of the more out-there communes, this sensual belonging can be as straightforward and polymorphously perverse as listening to the other. But it is a listening that is far from passive, it is an empathic and non-evaluative listening that can, in its offer of 'living attention', be sensual rather than instrumental. So, when Rancière writes that 'art lives as long as it expresses a thought unclear to itself in a matter that resists it', I feel we are more or less in the realms of an attentiveness to the *phônê*. The struggle to express is itself a marker of some kind of suffering. The resisting matter could, in some instances, be the logos, the unwieldy institution that often speaks on our behalf or which overwhelms us with its 'founding' status. When Rancière goes on to add '[art] lives inasmuch as it is something else than art', we could well be in the realm not only of child rearing, but also in the atopic space of the therapeutic relationship in which listening is orientated towards phases of singularity rather than carapaced 'selfs'.[24] Both these spaces are in many ways well distant from the polis and political discourse, but maybe it is here in the *phônétic* 'confusion of tongues', in the difficult disclosure of anxieties and of infra-psychic conflicts, in the 'heterogeneous sensible' of the self as a society, that there lies some chance of a redistrubution of the sensible; a 'metacategorical revolt' to cite Alexander Trocchi. For in both these spaces, as in many improvisatory musical spaces, there rings out another of Rancière's hopes for critical art as an 'art that questions its own limits and powers, that refuses to

---

23 Jacques Lacan, *The Seminar of Jacques Lacan Book I: Freud's Papers on Technique 1953-1954*, Cambridge: Cambridge University Press, 1988, p.218.

24 Rancière, *Dissensus*, op. cit., p.123.

anticipate its own effects.'[25]

This latter is maybe not something to herald so much as something to discover in the discontinuities of history, and it may explain Rancière's trap, as a much published cultural critic, to be compelled to speak of contemporary art. For such a 'refusal' as he envisions is already there in the radical indeterminacy of much surrealist practice; in the happenstance of contingent music, in a free improvisation willing to question idiom. But it is, one could hazard a guess, at play anywhere that there is a lack of conditionality and an openness to accept and treat as material the unconscious desires that animate and disable the potentially fluid metabolism of the 'heteregeneous sensible' of the social-psyche. This is the material (for better or for worse) through and from which group psychotherapy issues. So just as such a practice or concern could be ascribed to the partitioning of art as a separate sphere it could just as likely be de-partitioned to become, like it always was, the propensity of 'everybody and anyone at all'. This generic capacity, a facet of species-being caught in suffering in order to produce passion, could well be what is meant by 'class of sensitivity' or 'affective class', for in 'refusing to anticipate its own effects', in being beguiled by a candid expression of its own individualistic pitfalls, is it not that there is a refusal to reproduce the same confines for awareness? Does this refusal, based less on protective self-identification than on the mobility of affective states, entail an 'autotraumatic' embracing of the 'wilderness' of the psyche as a social microcosm? The traumas embedded in the past are maybe not so much indicators of personalised pathologies as potential insights into the ongoing social constructedness of each 'self' as it is pervertedly incarnated in history.

During an interview, pondering Marx's statement 'man produces man', Foucault commented: 'what must be

---

25 Ibid., p.149.

produced is not man identical to himself [...] we must produce something that doesn't yet exist and about which we cannot know."[26] Whether or not this 'existential possibility' could mean an evolved being to kick-start development beyond our being what Michael Balint has called 'neotenic embryos' is maybe not the point.[27] What is possibly at play in refusing to 'anticipate effects' is an acknowledgement of both how we may well be 'neotenic embryos' and how, 'leaning on' the offered commodity-props, we ward off the effects of contingency. From repressed memories to social planning, from routines and timetables to keeping our fingers crossed, from the recycling of acclaimed cultural moments to a risk-averse society what we are faced with is, as Adam Phillips writes, 'a history that our competence conceals'.[28] This history is one in which Marx and Freud collide: the necessity of an awareness of the past, to become historic beings in order to 'act out'. Rancière does make reference to works of the past as 'metamorphic elements', but we could suggest that our own pasts, the history of relationships that have formed us (some haphazard and personal, some determining and structural), are the Grand Narratives from which to embark on a 'redistirubution of the sensible'.[29] That these may resound with *phôné* is no reason, from the perspective of the polis, to denounce them as incoherent, animalistic and self-centred. The polis encourages all of these things.

June 2010

---

26 Michael Foucaul, *Power/Knowledge*, London: Harvester Press, 1980, p.121.
27 Michael Balint, *Primary Love and Psycho-Analytic Technique*, London: Karnac, 1985, p.133. 'Man (sic) can [...] be regarded as an animal which is retarded even in his "mature" age at an infantile form of love.'
28 Adam Phillips, op. cit., p.12.
29 Rancière, *Dissensus*, op. cit., p.125.

TWO UNTITLED POEMS

Two Untitled Poems

Untitled

Pre-anti-hope preposterous
operational bleed into Somalian
Sudan for sake of crooked
stink tank demos – deliver us
from national gender, sexual GNP,
racial insurance, sense tax.
Think speak of forbidden law.
Grow beyond the species burrow.

December 2002

Untitled

clinamens of
sensual difference
adumbrate
in slow motion
the evolution of
simple proposals

April 2010